LEARNING THROUGH PLAY

JAN NATANSON

WARD LOCK

A WARD LOCK BOOK

First published in the UK 1997
by Ward Lock
Wellington House
125 Strand
London WC2R 0BB
A Cassell Imprint

Distributed in the United States
by Sterling Publishing Co., Inc.
387 Park Avenue South, New York, NY 10016-8810

A British Library Cataloguing in Publication Data block for
this book may be obtained from the British Library

ISBN 0 7063 7623 4
Printed and bound by Dah Hua Printing Press Co.,
Hong Kong

Picture credits
Life File: 4, 6, 7, 10, 14, 24, 31, 33, 41, 47, 50–2, 57, 65, 67,
68, 71, 75, 76, 83, 98, 99, 104, 107, 109, 117, 118, 121

Reflections Photolibrary/Jennie Woodcock: 1, 5, 8–9, 13, 16,
17, 19–22, 27–31, 35, 39, 43, 44, 46, 48–9, 54, 55, 59–64,
69, 74, 77, 78, 80, 85, 86, 89–91, 93, 94–5, 97, 102, 105,
113–15, 123, cover

CONTENTS

INTRODUCTION

play and learning

A baby sitting in a highchair drops a toy onto the floor and watches with delight while someone picks it up again (and again and again). We see that the baby is playing, but what is he learning through such play? Dropping things for others to retrieve is not what most people would view as an important life skill or one that will be useful in later life.

However, it is through just such playful activity with objects and people that babies first explore their environment and come to understand their surroundings.

The baby in the highchair is exploring some of the physical properties of objects and experimenting with how they behave under different circumstances. Through such experimentation, he starts to gain some idea of physical laws. He is also exploring his own actions and ability to act upon the world. By experimenting with ideas such as cause and effect, a baby learns about the complex physical world that he is striving to make sense of. Such interaction between a baby's environment and his ability to act upon it underpins all his learning. This goes for his social environment as well. He is engaging with a caregiver and, through their interaction, extending his learning about social relationships and communication skills. It is through play that a baby comes to learn about the social world and his place within it.

Play is an enjoyable activity that carries its own reward. Babies engage with the world in a playful way quite naturally, but play can also be encouraged by a caregiver's attention and

approval. If caregivers encourage play, this builds up a baby's confidence for future playful explorations. He may be exploring, and acquiring concepts, testing out his ideas or practising skills as he plays. The important thing is that he is having fun and that any learning takes place as part of an enjoyable activity. Play is not training. It starts from the baby rather than being something imposed on the baby by others. By engaging in play activities, a baby learns not only particular behaviours but also, and perhaps more importantly, he employs a way of learning that is adaptable to changing environments and his own developing abilities.

At the same time, a caregiver may be able to extend and develop the learning potential of a baby's play activity. For example, our baby in a high chair might enjoy being given a variety of different objects to drop on the floor, including perhaps a feather which will float gently down instead of falling rapidly. This gives him a wider range of experiences from which to build up his understanding. Also, by talking about what is going on and emphasizing important words – '**Down** on the ground', '**Up** on the table' – a caregiver helps the baby in his learning about language and communication. But a lecture about gravity would probably do little to help a baby's understanding. In order to help the learning potential of play in the best possible way, it is important for a caregiver to be tuned into a baby's needs, to understand a bit about his abilities and how they develop as he grows.

A young scientist: this baby is enjoying the playful activity of dropping her toys from her high chair. Through such activities she learns about the world.

This baby shows great interest in the toys that he holds and all babies have an intense curiosity about the world of objects. Playing with toys is a serious learning experience for a baby.

DEVELOPMENTAL PROGRESS

Every baby is born an individual. He is born with his own genetic inheritance and he faces a unique set of influences and experiences through his life. He will have his own particular outlook on the world. This also means that he will mature and develop at his own pace. Some aspects of a baby's development depend solely or largely upon *maturation* – the rate at which the body and its processes mature. Others are influenced, to a greater extent, by what goes on in the child's environment and can vary with, for example, the amount of stimulation he receives or the input from his surroundings. All development involves an interaction between maturation and the effects of the environment.

The changes that occur as a child becomes an adult make up a very large area of study and child development can be broken down into the following different areas.

Motor development

Motor development refers to the development of movement and body control and co-ordination. Within this area, a useful distinction can be made between gross and fine motor skills. Gross motor skill refers to the large body movements and their control – such as walking. Fine motor skill refers to the small manipulative skills of finger and hand co-ordination involved with, for example, holding and exploring objects.

Cognitive development

Cognitive development refers to the development of mental processes such as thinking skills, memory and understanding as well as *perception* – the processing and interpreting of information

Babies often spend time in the kind of play that amounts to practice and mastery of different motor skills. Motor, cognitive and social skills are all intertwined in a child's developmental progress.

All children go through a similar sequence of developmental stages as they progress towards adulthood. But we have to remember that every child is an individual.

from the senses. Within an area such as cognitive development, some topics such as *language* and *communication skills* are sufficiently important to be dealt with as a separate area.

Social development

Social development refers to the development of a baby's social relationships, such as the building of strong emotional bonds with particular

individuals and also how he learns to find his place within the wider social network of society.

These areas are rarely separate or separable, however, when we consider the development of particular skills or abilities among children. The development of a particular behaviour may cross several areas of child development – for example, the development of language skills involves not only cognitive development (the ability to understand and process information), but also social development (a desire and ability to communicate) and motor development (the movement skills of the tongue needed to articulate words).

As a baby progresses towards adulthood, he goes through various stages of development. A stage refers to a broad descriptive category and reflects a range of particular abilities and skills. A particular stage is also usually associated with a certain chronological age in the baby or child. It is important to realize that, whenever ages are given in association with either the mastery of a particular skill or the progression to a developmental stage, these ages must be taken only as a very rough guide. Such ages are only averages and cover a very wide range of variation in 'normal', healthy and intelligent babies. Every baby is an individual. He may develop particular skills in a different order from other children. He will certainly develop at his own pace. If a caregiver has in mind a specific narrow and inflexible time-table about developmental progression, then this replaces the natural joy in a baby's achievement with anxiety and frustration which are unhelpful to a baby's development and sense of worth.

Why bother to give such indications of expected developmental progress? One reason is because it can be equally frustrating for caregivers and damaging to a child if we have totally unreal expectations of what he can understand or do at a certain stage in his development. Some understanding of what a child understands or what skills he may have at particular stages lessens the likelihood of such unrealistic expectations.

Another reason is that, if caregivers have some understanding of what skills or concepts a child is likely to acquire next, then this can inform the kind of interactions and choice of activities undertaken with the child. These activities then, in turn, feed back into a child's learning and influence his further development. What you do with a child depends not only on what you know he can do at the moment, but also on what you understand his expected skill progression to be.

SPECIAL NEEDS

Caring for all children requires much the same range of skills, one of the basic starting points always being to start from where the child is at. All caring for, teaching and playing with children start best from an intimate understanding of and empathy with the particular child. So a basic skill is an ability to see the world from the child's point of view. This helps a caregiver to adjust her own behaviour to mesh with a child's abilities and so allow the best kind of interaction for development.

Some children may be in especial need of a caregiver's help and understanding for a variety of reasons, if they are to interact with the world and develop their full potential. They may have

A baby signals his distress through crying. He lets his caregiver know he needs to be fed, changed or just to have some company.

Here the baby lies awake, alert to his surroundings and quite content to lie and gaze around him.

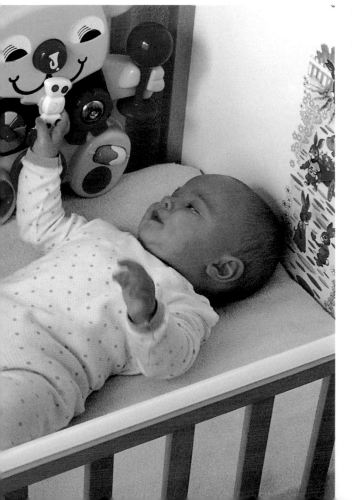

some mental or physical handicap that interferes with their ability to play and learn like other children. A child learns through activity and exploration, so anything that hampers these interferes with his developmental progress. If a caregiver cannot intervene to allow the child to play, explore and interact with his surroundings in whatever ways he can, then the initial handicap becomes compounded and has knock-on effects into his developmental progress. A child who cannot move very well is limited in his ability to explore his surroundings, test out his ideas in action and make discoveries about the world.

He may also be limited in interaction with other children. In this way the initial hurdle to normal playful engagement has knock-on effects on his cognitive and social development. A caregiver may have to help a child overcome physical limitations. The world may have to be brought to the child rather than the other way around. A caregiver may have to encourage a child to use whatever sense input he has to maximize his connection with both physical and social worlds.

Sometimes a child may be lacking in some of the strong intrinsic curiosity about the world that other children have, so that a caregiver may have to help motivate him to explore and play.

Starting from what a child is able to do, a caregiver has to establish what his special needs are. Sometimes these needs are the same as those for all children, but prolonged over time or increased in intensity.

Early establishment of special needs is very important if a child is to develop his full potential. Every child is an individual with a unique set of needs. Programmes of specialized skill training with special needs' children stress the establishment of a particular child's needs as a priority, and also the benefits of early intervention. Caregivers with an interest in special needs are recommended to contact particular national organizations that can give support, advice and recommendations on literature and programmes. There are some addresses on page 126 which may be useful. A detailed treatment of the topic lies outwith the scope of this book.

A MEMBER OF A SOCIETY

Increasingly, any study of children's development tends to stress the importance of social context as a framework within which to view all of a child's learning. Even the development of high-level thinking skills is grounded in a child's social world. As a child develops, his goal is, after all, to become a fully integrated and functioning member of a society.

The social context informs how babies learn. Social relationships are the base from which all

In cultures where babies are carried around, caregivers can respond directly and immediately to the changes in balance and small movements that signal a baby's discomfort and distress. Such close responsiveness results in babies who are more contented.

learning and development occur. He learns through interaction, observing and modelling the behaviour of those around him. As a baby, his environment is created by the people around him, and they mediate and control his interaction with it. Most importantly, it is within the emotional security of warm relationships that a baby is given the confidence to explore the wider physical environment.

Social context also informs what it is that children learn. Particular skills and behaviours that a child learns (including aspects of social relationships themselves) are very much grounded in the particular society or culture into which he is born. Different societies place different values on particular skills, behaviours and beliefs. Some things that are very important in one society may be irrelevant in another.

In the industrialized society of the West, with its more advanced technology and faster rates of change, we tend to prize certain skills. To function successfully as a member of such a society, a person needs to be capable of interacting and communicating effectively with a wide range of strangers. This is reflected in our great emphasis on acquiring verbal communication skills. In turn, this informs how we tend to interact with our babies and the importance we give to the early development of language skills in children. For other societies, other skills may be more valued and encouraged more.

CHILD-REARING PRACTICES

In the Western World, children are more segregated from adult activities. They have to learn information and practise skills in contexts that are not really the same as the usual grown-up situations. This has implications for how children learn. There tends to be more explicit teaching of skills by adults and an approach that focuses on the child. An adult takes responsibility for breaking down the mature skill in ways that help a child to learn.

In those cultures where there is more integration of children into adult activities, the responsibility for learning rests more with the child – who has to observe how the adult behaves and try to copy.

This difference can be seen in language learning. In some cultures, adults do not simplify their speech for children but act as models for the child to observe, listen and copy. In other cultures, adults take on a more active teacher role and simplify speech to children to help the learning process.

Within the scope of this book, cross-cultural aspects of child rearing cannot be treated with any depth. Some items are touched upon where they provide some interesting contrast or information that may inform more general topics of child development. But a shared culture of an advanced industrialized type is, for the most part, assumed among readers.

TERMINOLOGY

RATHER THAN USE 'he' or 'she' throughout the book when referring to babies, toddlers and children, I have used the convention of alternating 'he' and 'she' with each succeeding chapter. So in chapter one 'he' is used throughout, whereas in chapter two 'she' is used.

I hope this book will be of interest to a wide range of people involved in some way with babies and young children. They may be mothers, fathers, grannies, nursery workers, teachers, foster parents, child minders. As a result of this range, I have used the word 'caregiver(s)' to refer to the person(s) who look after the children. I use 'mother(s)' if referring to research in which the subjects are mothers. In later chapters, as a child's social horizons extend beyond the familiar, I use 'adults' to make the contrast with the close relationship of 'caregiver'.

CHAPTER ONE

THE NEWBORN

the first few months

AN INDIVIDUAL AND A SOCIAL BEING

A newborn baby is so fragile and helpless, compared with most other animals. To survive, he is totally dependent on the people around him. Social skills are the baseline survival skills of human beings, and in this respect the helpless human infant is already programmed for survival. It is no surprise that all adults, not just mothers, find the large eyes and disproportionately large head of babies appealing rather than strange. Similarly adults and children alike find the crying of babies a sound that they just cannot ignore.

The newborn baby is also, however, active in seeking to form social bonds with those around him, from the start. He has an inborn predisposition to establish himself as part of a social unit. He is a social being from birth.

A newborn baby is already very much an individual human being, with a particular mix of inherited genetic factors that influence his development and how he interacts with the world. Environmental factors play an equally important role in his development. The environment in the womb is crucial. We know from studies that fetal malnourishment, drugs and alcohol consumption by expectant mothers can have drastic and long-term effects on a baby's development. The state of health of a mother even before conception takes place can affect a baby's growth and development. So to give a baby the best possible start, it is vital to ensure that a mother's health is at its best both before and during pregnancy.

At birth a baby's brain is about twenty-five per cent of its adult weight and during the first year it reaches seventy per cent of its adult weight. Most of this growth does not involve an increase in the number of brain cells, but comes from the development of new nerve fibres and connections. Also the process by which the nerve fibres become coated in a fatty sheath, allowing faster and more reliable transmission of nerve impulses, proceeds rapidly at this early time of a child's life.

Lots of stimulation at this time of rapid growth can be particularly important as animal studies have shown that enriched environments can enhance brain growth and functioning.

TEMPERAMENT

Even at birth, babies have different temperaments. Some babies are naturally happier, or adapt easily to new circumstances. Others are more fussy and perhaps react more strongly emotionally. Babies can show differences in their normal behaviour patterns in terms of, for example: how well they respond to new things around them; how regular they are in terms of wanting to be fed, wanting to sleep and needing to be changed; how much time they spend awake and alert; and how much fussing, fretting and restlessness they may show. These different patterns have enabled psychologists to classify them into broad temperamental categories.

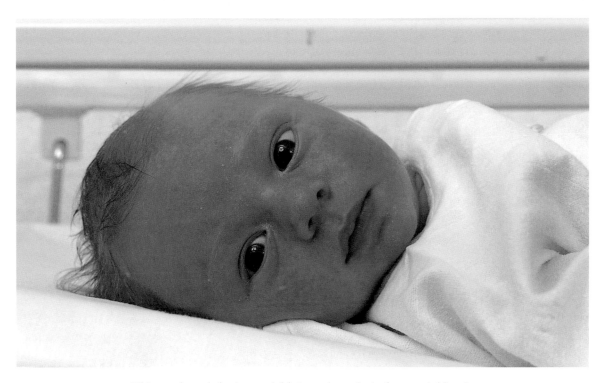

This newborn baby is a social being – he seeks to form social bonds from the start.

Temperamental differences have a strong effect on a baby's interactions with the world and other people. These interactions can, in turn, feed back to strengthen particular temperaments. A sunny happy baby usually has the kind of interactions that reinforce his happy nature.

Some broad temperament patterns, such as sociability, irritability, activity level and emotionality, have been found to persist and remain fairly constant throughout life. Other temperament characteristics are, however, influenced much more by external factors. One major environmental influence is the parent's own temperament.

A mother with a particular temperament might herself expect a broadly similar temperament in her baby. Parents' expectations of how they think a baby should act influences how they respond to the baby's temperament. The match or mismatch between parent and baby can either support or modify aspects of a child's temperament.

The main thing must, however, be to make a baby feel accepted and wanted. All development should be built on that secure foundation. A baby isn't a blank thing to be moulded. He is a person from the start – an individual – but also a social being who can only develop and grow within a secure social network.

Sometimes a baby, by his temperament, tends to be more anxious and fretful, and when he is awake he may cry frequently. All babies, however, even those of the sunniest disposition, signal their discomfort through crying.

Crying usually signals hunger, pain or discomfort, but often a baby continues to cry even when the cause has been alleviated. A baby's first need after food is for human contact. For his emotional development, a baby needs to develop trust in his caregivers that they will pay attention to his cries and try to comfort him. Before a baby can start to explore the world, he needs to feel comfortably alert. If he is in distress, what can a caregiver do to comfort him?'

COMFORT TECHNIQUES

Holding, cuddling and stroking: these are the primary comfort techniques. Despite old wives' tales of babies being spoiled by attention, responding quickly to a baby's distress leads to less crying. It has been found that babies who are left to cry become more demanding and fretful.

Swaddling: it can sometimes help a fretful baby to wrap him firmly in a shawl or sheet. The swaddling stops any involuntary movement of the baby's limbs which might interfere with falling asleep in a tired baby. Studies have shown that swaddled babies not only sleep more but also spend more of their wakeful time actively alert.

Voices, music or low-frequency sounds (such as a Hoover): these can help soothe a crying baby. For newborn babies the sound of a *heartbeat* can often help recreate a kind of womb comfort.

Rocking: rocking, at the rate of about sixty ups and downs per minute, can also help some babies. Again rocking probably recreates a similar feeling to movement experienced in the womb.

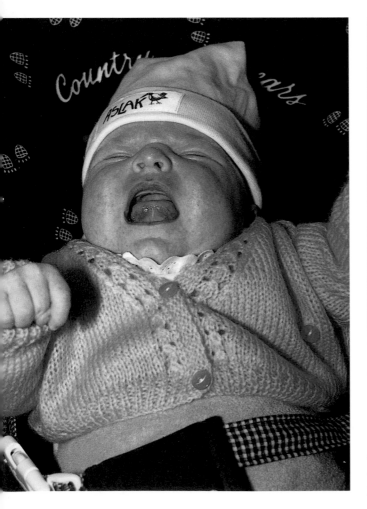

Babies do vary in temperament from the moment that they are born. Some are more irritable, anxious and emotional, whereas others seem much happier in disposition. Such differences in temperament may persist throughout a person's life.

THE WORLD OF THE NEWBORN BABY

A newborn baby may be quite helpless in many respects but he is anything but inactive. From the start, he is not just the passive receiver of input from his surroundings. He learns through interacting with his bright new world, and he has a drive to interact from the word go.

His limited ability to move means, however, that he has less control over his interaction than he will develop later. His learning from and engagement with the external world depend on the development of his senses and perception. It also depends upon the caregiver(s) in two important ways. His caregivers make up a baby's social and emotional world, and also bring the wider external world of objects and experiences to the baby. By knowing where a baby is at, they can mediate what aspects of the wider world he can interact with.

A newborn baby already has the kind of predisposition that helps him start to make sense of the world around him. From the start, a baby takes an active part in his own learning – learning about his world through his own senses.

In terms of brain maturation, the first nerve cells to be fully insulated (and therefore able to transmit nerve impulses quickly) are those associated with the sense organs, and is one reason why a baby's senses work almost as well as those of adults after only a few short months.

It is also important for a baby to have plenty of sensory experience in the first few months in order to develop all the senses.

Sight

At birth babies can see but not very well – they have some visual discrimination but will not see things sharply. They can focus only within a narrow range of about ten to twelve inches (just the right distance for viewing the face of the person who is feeding them). A baby's visual perception develops rapidly in the first few months. Initially, a caregiver has to bring things into his range of focus, so mobiles and other toys should be positioned with this in mind. With experience a baby's eyes learn to focus both closer and further away. A baby learns to see through looking, so visual stimulation is important.

What does a baby like to look at? There have been a lot of studies on the visual perception of young babies. We now know that babies like to look at moving objects more than immobile ones, and prefer slow movements to fast ones. They prefer certain colours, such as red. They prefer curved shapes and, at least to start with, seem to attend more to the outlines of things than to the inner detail. Edges of high contrast appeal, which explains partly why they like faces so much – they like the contrast of light and shade at the hairline and eyes. Faces are very appealing for babies.

So young babies enjoy looking at brightly coloured, slowly moving objects within their visual range. This makes mobiles a good early toy. When choosing one keep the baby's viewpoint in mind. If the mobile is viewed from below, then the interesting features should be visible from that angle. Babies like high contrast and they enjoy the play of a torch beam on a dark ceiling or dark shapes on a white background. They like looking at new things, so perhaps it is better to have a high turnover of home-made mobiles than to invest in expensive equipment, the characteristics of which appeal more to adults than to babies.

As a baby's visual perception develops over the first few months, they show a preference for increasingly complex patterns. They learn to discriminate between colours, for example, by two months they can tell red from green.

In the first few months, babies begin to learn to track things with their eyes. Initially, they are unable to track a moving object smoothly. At two months, their eyes tend to follow in a series of jerky movements. A caregiver can help this development by showing objects, attracting a baby's attention by positioning the object right in front of his face and perhaps moving it a bit.

A newborn baby can focus best at a distance of about twelve inches – just right for watching the face of whoever is feeding him.

Once you have got the baby's visual attention, you can then try to get him to follow the object as you move it first to one side and then to the other. This has to be paced to allow time for the baby to focus and moved slowly enough for his eyes to follow. As with all games, a baby soon lets you know when he doesn't want to play any more.

Hearing

By the time he is born, a baby has been listening in for some time to a muffled version of what's going on in the outside world. We know that newborn babies prefer listening to their own mother's voice, rather than other female voices, which shows that they have already learned to recognize it while still in the womb. Newborn babies have even been shown to prefer listening to the particular rhyme that their mother had sung repeatedly to them during the last few weeks before their birth. After birth the babies preferred to listen to the particular rhyme 'Mary had a little lamb' which they had heard before birth to another nursery rhyme, again sung by their own mother but not heard before (De Casper and Fifer, 1980).

So this is perhaps something that expectant parents might like to try out for themselves. A particular piece of music could be played regularly to the baby in the last few weeks before he is born. In the first few days after birth, hearing something familiar might be soothing. Perhaps making a tape of his mother's voice singing the song or reading the story might help during periods when she cannot be with the baby.

Young babies have quite well developed hearing at birth. They turn towards the source of a sound from early on. Even two-day-old babies have been seen to move their heads towards the sound of a rattle, but they do this more slowly than older children or adults. This ability to locate a sound's source is a skill that develops rapidly during a baby's first months of life.

For the first few months, babies use the difference in loudness of the sound at each ear to make judgements about direction. At about four months, babies use the difference in timing of a sound arriving at each ear to locate a sound source, which allows for even greater accuracy. Such time differences amount to only thousandths of a second, so in a short time the baby's auditory perception makes great developmental strides.

As with visual tracking, you can use bells or

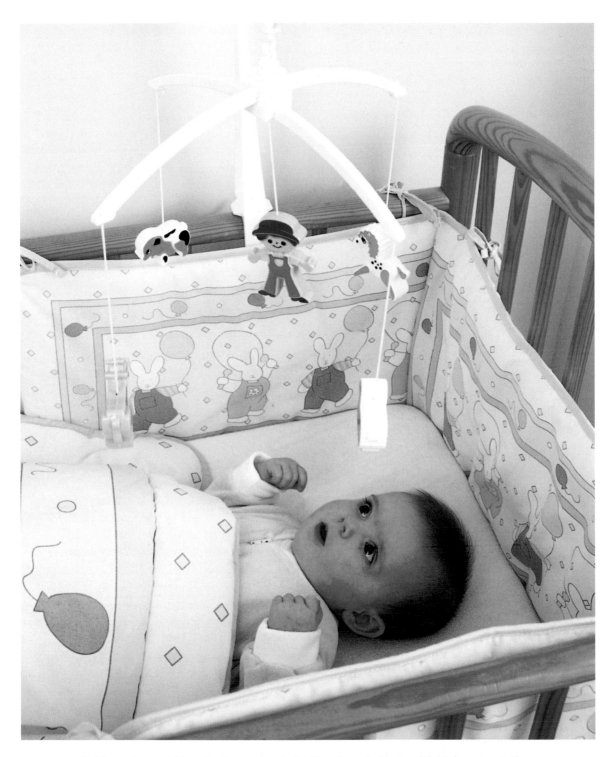

Babies enjoy watching slowly moving, brightly coloured objects with high contrast; they also like faces and patterns. Mobiles like this one make a good early toy. They also like looking at new things, so it is a good idea to have various home-made mobiles that can be swapped around.

rattles to play sound-tracking games. Small bells make a high-pitched noise which babies seem to like; babies usually attend more to higher-pitched sounds. As they seem more sensitive to such sounds, they are better at locating them.

First, try to get the baby's attention, then move the bell slowly from one side to the other, and then see if he makes any movement in the direction of the bell. Or you can try with two differently pitched bells. Don't be disappointed if you don't get much of a reaction, however. Babies differ in their temperaments and in the amount of time that they spend in a state of wakeful alertness in which they can interact in this way. Newborn babies also differ in their ability to notice and attend to things in their surroundings. The main thing is always to start from where the baby is at, which means not only his developmental level but also his own particular state of alertness and desire to interact.

Babies like listening to music especially if it has a strong rhythm. As with all sounds in their environment, it must not, however, startle them.

Speech

Babies show a preference for patterned sound compared with single tones and they prefer those patterns that lie within the frequency range of human speech. They have a particular propensity to tune into speech sounds. They attend more to voices than to other sounds in their environment, and seem to have an innate predisposition to focus on selective features of spoken language; for example, they listen more to a voice that is directed to another baby than one directed to another adult, which shows that they are sensitive to the particular acoustic properties of this speech, such as higher pitch and slower tempo. At only four days, it has been shown that babies can discriminate between their native language and non-native language (Cooper and Aslin, 1994).

So it is of prime importance that caregivers talk to babies. The language that babies hear around them, especially the language that is directed at them in particular, forms the environment necessary for a baby to begin learning language right from the start.

Taste and smell

From the beginning, babies seem to be able to discriminate smells – they turn their heads from bad smells like rotten fish but not from pleasant odours. Breast-feeding newborn babies can also distinguish the smell of their own mother's milk from that of another nursing mother on a pad. They can do this when they are six days old, but not at two days, which would suggest that such discrimination has been learned in those few short days. From birth, babies show a distinct preference for sweet tastes over sour or bitter ones.

Touch

For a long time it was thought that newborn babies were insensitive to pain, which is not the case. In fact, the latest research shows that, even at an early stage in the womb, they can feel pain. Babies are very sensitive to touch. Many of the reflexes that they are born with involve responding to touch on particular parts of their body. If touched on the cheek, a baby turns his head, if touched on the lips he starts to suck and, if stroked on the soles of his feet, his toes fan out.

It is important for a baby's well-being to be held and touched. Holding, stroking and cuddling are the most common ways of comforting a crying baby. Some fretful newborn babies respond to gentle massage. Touch plays an important part in social bonding.

For a baby, the process of attachment begins with the communication of mutual touch, long before he can understand language or talk himself. Secure attachment is the baseline from which all developmental progress is made.

When a baby is distressed, he needs to be comforted. Gentle stroking is often very effective as babies are very sensitive to touch. This baby is being comforted through such stroking.

REFLEXES

Newborn babies show several inborn, automatic responses to stimuli. Some of these, such as *breathing*, *blinking* and *swallowing*, are retained throughout life. Others develop and change into patterns of behaviour that are more under a baby's voluntary control. For examples of the reflexes see the box.

Playing with a baby's reflexes

Obviously, no caring adult would wish to keep startling a newborn baby just to see the Moro reflex, or throw him in the deep end just to see him swim. Some reflexes do, however, develop and become incorporated into a baby's regularly used behaviours for interacting with and finding out about the world. These can be the basis for the first joint explorations of a caregiver and a baby. Alongside the more essential interactions during feeding, nurturing and comforting, caregivers can play with a baby from the start.

Walking

Studies have shown that practice of this walking reflex does have some effect on the development of later walking skills, although it is not clear exactly how this happens. If a baby shows a stepping reflex, a caregiver might like to try encouraging him to practise it. The emphasis must be on curiosity and play rather than any idea of training or exercise, however.

This action is one of the behaviours in the baby's repertoire and so he might enjoy the experience of the sensation. The main thing is to be responsive to the baby. He will communicate whether he is happy or not.

Grasping

The grasping reflex can be the starting point for first games of give and take, long before true voluntary reaching and grasping appear among the baby's skills.

When the baby is alert and comfortable, try getting his attention with a small easily held

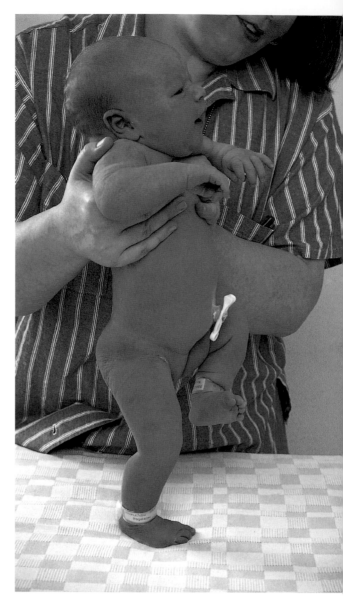

The stepping reflex is one that babies have until they are about eight weeks old. As shown here, babies, held under the arms with the soles of their feet just touching a solid flat surface, will often lift their legs in a walking or stepping motion.

The grasping reflex is demonstrated when a small object or mother's finger is placed in a baby's palm. He closes his palm and his fingers curl around in a firm grasp. This reflex usually lasts three months.

REFLEXES

Sucking reflex: any object causes sucking if it intrudes into a baby's mouth. This develops into mouthing behaviour whereby a baby uses his mouth to find out about the properties of objects. Other reflexes seen in newborn babies disappear within a short period of time and also in a particular sequence that shows a developmental progression. Both the appearance and disappearance of these reflexes at predictable time intervals reflect the underlying development of the baby's nervous system and show that such development is normal.

Stepping reflex: a newborn baby, if held under the arm in an upright position and with the base of his foot just touching a solid surface such as a table-top or a floor, will step with his feet as if walking. This reflex disappears by about eight weeks of age, although it has been found to take a little longer to disappear if the reflex is practised. Newborn babies who are held upright so as to stimulate the stepping reflex learn to walk earlier than average, even though the reflex had since disappeared (Zelazo et al., 1972).

Rooting reflex: if a baby is touched on the cheek, his head turns to that side. The baby is searching for a nipple. This disappears by six months.

Grasping reflex: if something is placed in a baby's hand, then his palm closes and his fingers curl around it in a firm grasp. This reflex tends to disappear around three months of age.

Swimming reflex: if put into water, a baby holds his breath and moves his arms and legs. This disappears by four to six months.

Babinski reflex: when the bottom of a baby's foot is stroked, the toes fan outwards and then curl. This reflex disappears between eight and twelve months.

Moro reflex: in response to a loud noise, a baby throws out his arms and opens his fingers as he arches back. The arching disappears by six months, but a modified startle reaction persists throughout life.

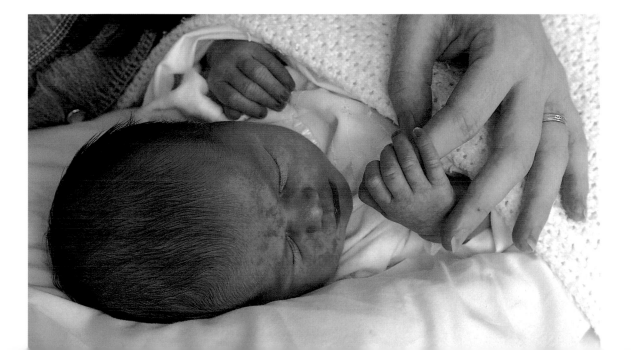

rattle, then move it slowly towards him and place it in his hand, so that his grasping reflex holds it firmly. With both of you holding on to the rattle, try moving his arm so that he can enjoy making a noise. (In fifteen years' time you might wonder why you ever bothered!) Of course, at this stage, you are doing all the work, but by exercising his early grasping reflex he is starting on the path of exploring the world of objects.

Babies like to grasp hold of any small object – adult fingers being a favourite – and this can be the start of little social games between a caregiver and a baby, which are the basis for all learning of language and communication. Babies soon learn to recognize the intonation patterns of speech that signify positive emotions and the little rituals of repeated actions and vocal signals. Finger-grasping games can soon develop into the

kind of one-to-one routines that are the ideal learning situations for encouraging a baby's social, emotional and cognitive development.

You can also play finger games with your baby which involve uncurling his grasping fingers so as to tickle or stroke his palm. Development often involves a baby learning to inhibit earlier behaviours or reflexes.

EARLY IMITATION

Even very young babies can show some kinds of behaviour that seem to exhibit much more advanced skills than we give them credit for. One such behaviour is imitation.

Babies of less than four days have been shown to be capable of imitating an adult who was opening his mouth and sticking out his

This young baby is responding to his mother's expression by imitating it. Very young babies can sometimes carry out these early imitations in response to a range of exaggerated adult expressions such as tongue pokes, pouts, etc. This early imitation doesn't last long.

tongue (Meltzoff and Moore, 1983). Two-day-old babies could imitate a smile, a pout and a surprised open mouth. How can they do this? Some have suggested a reflex, and certainly imitation is seen only in the very youngest of the babies studied. Researchers studying slightly older babies found no evidence of early imitation. So perhaps it is a reflex that disappears within the first few days of life. A reflex normally means that it is an automatic behaviour exhibited by all babies, but imitation does not fit with this. Not all babies show early imitation and, even among imitators, they do not always show this behaviour.

Others have suggested that humans have an inborn ability to imitate the actions of others, or that this early imitation is part of a newborn baby's inborn organizational scheme – how he is wired up to perceive the world. In this early organizational scheme, perception of actions and their production are bound together.

INTEGRATION OF SENSORY INPUT

Babies turn towards the source of a sound, and they turn in response to touch. Babies of one month seem to connect the sense of touch with vision. Studies showed that they looked more at a picture of either a smooth or a bumpy dummy depending on which kind they had been sucking on (Meltzoff and Borton, 1979).

Babies do therefore seem to be actively involved in putting together information from all the senses, in order to make sense of the world. This integration of the senses starts from the earliest days. Babies soon put a voice and face together to recognize the people closest to them, and they do this not only when the real people are present. For example, studies show that within three weeks a baby looks at photographs of his mother more if a recording of his mother's voice is playing at the same time.

When a bit older, a baby looks at a film that matches a soundtrack more than one that

doesn't. The speed with which babies learn to do this means that, from the start, they must be integrating, organizing and comparing sensory data. In fact, it may be the case that some kinds of perceptual processing are linked together to start with and only later become differentiated.

EARLY MEMORY

From very early on, babies recognize the familiar and are captivated by the new. This behaviour, called habituation, whereby a baby pays attention to something new for a while then gets bored with it and stops paying attention, implies that they must somehow be able to store information about the world. Otherwise, how could they know that something has not been seen before?

It has been shown that a newborn baby recognizes his mother's voice from before birth and even recognizes a particular rhyme read to him in the last few weeks before birth. This evidence of early memory implies an ability to process and store sensory information. From the start, babies are active in their own learning in terms of how (the process) and what (the content) they take in from the outside world.

SMILES

The baseline survival skills for humans are the social and emotional skills needed to form attachment to other people. The newborn baby has some inborn reflexes which help him, and he quickly learns other social skills. The smile is one of a baby's best survival weapons. Even an exhausted sleep-deprived parent, in the middle of changing a particularly disgusting nappy, can forgive everything for a glimpse of the fleeting exercise of a baby's facial muscles that we call a smile.

Over the first few weeks and months of life, a baby's smiling develops. The very first fleeting smiles tend to occur only when the baby is sleeping. It is thought to be a response to the neural stimulation that occurs during rapid eye movement (REM) sleep. This is the kind of light sleep associated, in adults, with dreaming. It is characterized by a particular brain wave pattern and the rapid movements that the eyeballs tend to make beneath closed eyelids, which show that dreaming is occurring. These first smiles don't happen very often and when they do they don't last very long.

After a couple of weeks, external stimulation can also make a baby smile and he is more likely to smile when he is alert. Gentle stimulation, such as ringing a bell or shaking a rattle, may make him smile, but he is most responsive to hearing a human voice. After a month, a baby smiles more often and does so in response to social stimulation. He smiles most when he hears a female voice.

At six weeks of age, there is a change. Instead of a voice, it is the human face that is most effective in bringing out the smiles in a

Smiling is a baby's best survival weapon and at six weeks this develops into a proper 'smile'. This baby is smiling in response to his favourite stimulus – a human face with its edges of high contrast.

baby. The smile itself starts to change. It now involves cheek and eye muscles, as well as those of the mouth. It is a seen by adults as a proper smile. The smile lasts longer and a baby comes out with more of them.

Six weeks seem to mark some developmental stage. Many studies have noticed that it is the conceptual age (the age measured from a baby's conception) of forty-six weeks that is associated with a baby starting to smile at faces. So, for example, a premature baby born four weeks early will probably not start smiling at faces until ten weeks of age. This seems to reinforce the idea that starting to smile at faces reflects some development in maturation, rather than being dependent on experience during the early weeks after birth (Bower, 1977).

A smile, by this stage, has become a social behaviour that is rewarded by adult approval and a smiling adult response. Very rapidly, smiling becomes the currency of social interchange – a behaviour that carries its own social and emotional rewards. A caregiver can win smiles regularly by behaving in a certain way. The baby gradually learns to distinguish people and smiles more at those he knows. The smile is an important social behaviour signalling positive emotions and is the building block of a baby's growing communication with those around him.

Cause and effect

Lots of things make a baby smile: being tickled, being spoken to by a caregiver, and certain noises and sensations. As the baby develops, however, there is one class of event that he finds more and more satisfying. These are associations between events or one thing following on from another in a reliable predictable way. From very early on, a baby gets pleasure from making things happen. Initially, most movements that he makes tend to be random. He moves his arms and kicks his legs for no purpose other than the sensation of movement. Babies are very quick to notice patterns – they are a part of the way in which they make sense of the world they

are born into. So, if a certain arm movement seems to bring about a certain effect, they learn to repeat that movement to recreate the effect. This is the way a baby's crying pattern changes in the first few months. At first crying is a direct involuntary response to a baby's internal state. The baby has no control over his crying, he is simply reacting directly to what he feels. He soon learns that a cry is followed by the appearance of a caregiver. Gradually, the cry changes to become a signal. A baby sometimes stops crying, not when the discomfort is alleviated, but as soon as the caregiver appears.

Towards the end of these first few months a caregiver might like to see if a baby enjoys playing around with cause-and-effect events. Some babies have to be a little bit older before they enjoy such things, because in the early months babies vary in the amount of stimulation they enjoy.

BABY GAMES

YOU CAN TIE a balloon to a baby's wrist with a ribbon so that his arm movements cause it to bob around. He should find this interesting, especially if the balloon is shiny or patterned, or has a face drawn on it. You could try tying bells to his ankles, so his kicking legs are rewarded by a pleasant sound, or filling the end of his cot with crumpled paper which makes a nice rustling noise as he kicks against it. As with all early games with young babies, the main thing is to be responsive to his desires. A tired baby may not enjoy being stimulated in this way. It is also important to be alert to a baby's safety, which means enjoying these activities together. For a baby, this is the most satisfying pattern of all – the presence of a caring adult whose face, smile and voice become an integral part of his enjoyable interaction with the world.

CHAPTER TWO

THE YOUNG INFANT

three to six months

Starting to take her place

By this stage, although still sleeping a lot, a baby is starting to be awake for increasingly longer periods of time. (Not only in the middle of the night – it just might seem like that to bleary eyed parents.)

She is becoming more interested in the world around her and more eager to engage with it. Her developing perceptual skills and growing control over her movements mean that she can direct herself better to whatever interests her in her environment. She can also interact more with those around her and can do so for longer periods of time. This, of course, in turn affects her developing perceptual and motor skills. Suddenly, a baby's learning about the world starts to accelerate as she changes into a higher gear.

DEVELOPING RELATIONSHIPS

Growing attachment to caregivers

A baby is a social being from birth. In many ways she is programmed to make herself a part of human society. Initially, however, she does not really discriminate between the different people with whom she may interact. She interacts and smiles with everyone. Only over time does she begin to differentiate between people and start to prefer some to others.

She starts to develop a special relationship or bond with only one or two particular people – normally those who look after her most often. This process, called *attachment*, is possibly the most important development that takes place at this time because it underpins all other developmental progress, not only in the sphere of social and emotional growth, but also in cognitive development.

At one time it was thought that there was a critical period for *attachment* just after birth and that it was important for the bonding process for mothers and their newborn babies to be together at that time. This has now been shown to be less important. What are important are the close interactions between a baby and her caregiver – the talking, feeding, cuddling and nurturing. It is through these interactions that a bond grows. A baby develops a sense of trust that her needs will be met and that she will receive warmth, care and attention. It is in this way that an enduring relationship are built up.

A strong bond is very important. It is the foundation upon which all future relationships with others are built. It is the baseline for a baby's social and emotional growth, although the relationship also affects other aspects of her development. A secure relationship does not restrict a child's other interactions, but rather helps to encourage them. It has been shown in studies that babies who are strongly attached to a caregiver show more active exploratory behaviour than those who are not so securely attached. Also infants reared in institutions

At this stage a baby develops a special relationship with her caregivers and those close to her. This process of attachment is very important.

showed less curiosity than home reared infants when presented with something new. A secure attachment to a caregiver can give a baby the confident base from which she can then explore the wider world.

DEVELOPING MOTOR CONTROL

A baby makes great progress in the control of her own body at this time. Gradually she learns to sit up unsupported. By four months, a baby usually needs support under the arms otherwise she falls over. By six months, she can usually balance in a sitting position as long as there is some support at tummy level. By the end of her seventh month, a baby can usually sit by herself without help.

By six months, some babies are able to move by rolling over – if placed on a flat surface on their fronts they can roll over onto their backs.

Making a grab at the world

By three months, babies have increased muscle strength. Babies at this stage seem to enjoy spontaneous movement for its own sake. She enjoys waving her arms or kicking her legs just for the sensation, rather than for any consequence of that movement. Initially, these movements are not under her control and only with development can she learn to direct her movements towards particular ends or goals. What are a baby's goals? At this age they are anything and everything in her surroundings that attracts her attention. She is most interested in people and especially those people whom she has begun to know. At this young age, toys are usually only of any interest to her if they are played with by a caregiver. It is play with the caregiver that she enjoys, the toys just being an accompaniment to the interaction.

Joint attention

It is a good idea to play in this way with young babies, using a toy as the focus of a game. Developing a shared focus or joint attention between a caregiver and a baby provides an ideal situation for shared communication, and this kind of shared focus later helps a baby to learn about shared meanings. This also helps in the development of her language skills. Studies have shown that mothers who more frequently encourage their four-month-old babies to attend to particular objects, or events in their immediate surroundings, tend to have babies with larger speaking vocabularies at twelve months. Research has also shown that when mothers were encouraged to increase these kind of interactions, in which they tried to focus their babies' attention on something, this had an effect on the babies' own behaviour even two months later. Those babies whose attention was focused in this way tended to show more competence when exploring their surroundings on their own (Belsky, Goode and Most, 1980).

Using a toy as a focus, this caregiver is sharing a focus of attention with her baby. This creates an ideal situation for learning about shared meanings and for developing language skills through communication.

A more upright position may aid babies in their ability to reach for objects.
Reaching behaviour is important for exploring the environment and
developing motor co-ordination.

Palm grip

A baby can hold onto objects well at this stage, although not if they are too small. Although she may have lost her early grasping reflex, when she holds onto something she still uses the same kind of grip – holding the object in the palm of her hand with her fingers curled around. She holds the object quite securely but may drop it if she sees something else that she wants to hold instead. As soon as it has fallen, the object ceases to exist as far as she is concerned. It is very much a case of 'out of sight, out of mind'.

Reach for it

A lot of reaching behaviour reflects the maturation of the central nervous system. But studies of reaching behaviour among young babies have, however, shown the important effect that body position can have. They have found that infants of three to four and a half months held in a vertical position showed reaching behaviour equivalent to that shown by infants of five to eight and a half months in other positions. The former showed more reaches and had a better aim and success rate than babies in a prone position (Savelsbergh and Van der Kamp, 1994). Being in an upright position meant that a baby's ability to reach was enhanced and her performance improved.

Reaching is a basic exploration behaviour and one that carries the potential for its own reward. If a baby successfully reaches for something, she is encouraged to reach again and again. She can start to control her exploration of her immediate environment. This produces a learning loop which feeds back into her developing skills and accelerates her learning about both her environment and her own body control.

Fingers and toes are endlessly fascinating – as this baby discovers. At the same time, babies are busy learning to integrate sensory input from touch, movement and sight.

Fingers and toes

One of the most fascinating things for a young baby is her own fingers. She looks at them, grabs hold of them, interlaces them and explores them with her mouth. She is learning about her fingers and what they can do and integrating the input from touch, movement and sight. Cross-cultural studies have shown that Mexican infants who play a lot with their fingers because they do not have other toys are more advanced in manipulative skills than American infants.

Mouthing

The early sucking reflex now develops into mouthing behaviour, which is one of the main ways in which a baby explores her world. Mouthing is not exactly the same as indiscriminate sucking. In mouthing, a baby uses different sucking movements to explore different materials, so her mouth takes on a different shape depending on whether it is her finger or her blanket that she is exploring. A baby's mouth is very sensitive. By mouthing an object, she is able to extract a wide variety of information about texture, shape and size. It is important for her development that she has access to a wide variety of different objects. Knowing that one of her primary means of exploration is by mouthing, caregivers have to chose and select carefully what the baby can explore. Obviously, safety must be a first concern along with considerations of hygiene and durability. Thought should perhaps also be given to what kind of experience a baby will have in exploring a particular object if that exploration is by mouth. A wide variety of shapes and textures is as important as solely visual considerations like colour.

TOYS AND GAMES FOR PLAY AND DEVELOPMENT

People, people and more people! The best toys for a baby at this stage are caring adults who will hold, cuddle, talk, touch, sing, smile, make faces at her, respond to her, engage her attention and play turn-taking games such as 'peek-a-boo'.

Things to look at: such as people, mobiles (brightly coloured, high contrast and with increasingly complex patterns to suit a baby's developing visual preferences), mirrors (non-breakable and easily held), cardboard or cloth picture books.

Things to hold, touch, explore by hand or mouth: objects and toys with a variety of textures, sizes, shapes, colours and materials. Often baby toys tend to be very similar in texture – all made of plastic. But the sense of touch is very important. Mouthing behaviour develops from the early sucking reflex. Through a variety

of different sucking movements this baby can explore an object in her hand and obtain a great deal of information.

Things to listen to: tapes of voices, songs, rhymes, music for when the real thing is not available. Rattles, bells, crumpled paper, especially when baby makes the noise herself.

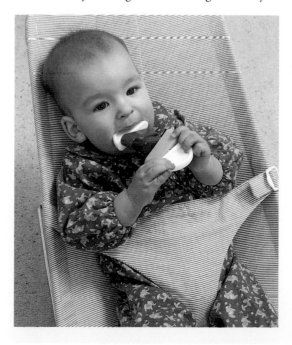

Water play: bath time gives baby the opportunity to experience a variety of different tactile sensations and different movement experiences. It also allows the baby the opportunities for exploration of objects in different ways.

Games with caregivers: physical play, for example, bouncing games such as 'This is the way the farmer rides'; social /language play, for example, turn-taking games, 'Round and round the garden', 'Peek-a-boo'.

DEVELOPING SENSES

Tuning into language

A baby can now increasingly discriminate between sounds. She can tell where they come from with increasing accuracy. Experience of listening to the language around her, and being talked to means that she has started to discriminate the patterns of speech which will be important for her later linguistic development. For example, she can already discriminate between phonemes, that is, the basic sounds of a language. She can tell the difference between 'pa' and 'ba' long before she can produce those different sounds herself. In fact, as babies get older and have more and more experience of listening to particular language sounds, they start to lose some of their earlier ability to discriminate those sounds not actually used in their native language. They gradually focus more sharply on the sounds that are needed and lose the ability to discriminate those that aren't.

One study showed that, in an English-speaking community, babies of six to eight months old could distinguish the consonant contrasts present in the Hindi language. By age twelve months, however, the same babies could no longer detect the differences (Werker and Tees, 1985).

Babies may have some inborn abilities to perceive language, but these are modified by the language that the baby hears around her.

Understanding voices

A baby already recognizes the voices of care-givers, and she can soon learn to put voices and faces together. For example, when a baby's mother and father are both present, if a tape recording of father's voice is played she turns towards him, whereas if a recording of mother's voice is played then she turns her face towards her mother.

Babies very quickly come to take in the patterns of what they hear as they try to make sense of everything around them; voices soon come to be associated with particular people.

Particular aspects of voices also have associated meanings for a baby. For example, even at this age, she is very much aware of those features of voices that convey emotional content. This happens long before she can understand the actual meaning of the spoken words. Both the inflection patterns that signify positive emotions and those that signify negative ones are recognized. Babies are aware of approval and disapproval in a caregiver's tone of voice and respond appropriately from about five months. Studies have shown that a baby is aware of approval or disapproval in voices, even when speaking in languages other than the baby's own native language. For example, when babies from English native-speaking homes were spoken to in Italian or German, or even nonsense English, they were still aware of the emotional content of what was being said (although not so aware for Japanese speaking voices) (Fernald, 1993).

At the same age, babies cannot reliably read emotions from facial expressions alone. But if sad or happy faces had the appropriate vocal tone accompanying them, then babies were able to respond correctly.

Seeing things

The idea of object constancy

When we look at a single object, several images can hit our retinas, and these images vary in many different ways. Different light conditions mean that the colour information hitting our eyes varies. Similarly, the angle that we view it at, how the object itself is positioned and how far away it is all mean that different images are being sent to the eye and yet our brains perceive it as the one object.

When that object moves all the images change again – yet again we still see it as the same object.

This ability to perceive objects as constants is something that a baby starts to learn from very early on.

Babies enjoy seeing the world from different angles. This baby is enjoying a view of the big wide world, from the security of close contact with mum.

Size and shape constancy

One kind of constancy that a baby has to learn is related to size. She has to understand that a far away object is not small (despite the small image that hits her retina), but a large object at a distance.

Another feature of objects is their shape. The perceived shape depends on the angle that the object is viewed from and this can vary with different viewing angles. So any movement of a head will cause the perceived shape to change. A baby has to learn that objects have their own intrinsic shape, which is constant and does not vary with the angle of perception. She has to learn that a cup is a cup if seen from the side or the top or underneath. Babies start to acquire this idea of shape constancy from around three months, although at this age usually only for very simple shapes.

Even though babies may be born with built-in frameworks for organizing perceptions, they need to have a wide experience of looking at different shapes and objects in order to develop these perceptual abilities. This is where a wide and rich variety of things to look at is very important for babies. It is also important to have different viewpoints. It helps babies to see the world from different angles – carried around in slings or backpacks, or propped up in baby-safe, semi-upright and upright chairs.

Depth perception

When do babies first perceive depth? The ability to perceive depth is very important for the development of a baby's ability to reach for and grasp objects. If you can't tell how far away something is, the chances are, if you make a grab for it, then you might not be successful.

Researchers have used the *visual cliff* apparatus to test a baby's ability to see depth. This consists of a clear glass platform over a drop so that, although the baby can safely crawl all over the surface, half of it shows an apparent drop. It has been found that even two-month-old babies showed an increased heart rate when placed on the 'cliff side' compared with the 'non-cliff' side. For young babies, an increased heart rate is associated with interest rather than fear, so they must be aware, at some level, of a difference between the two sides – sufficient difference to create interest. It probably makes sense that there is some rudimentary perception of depth at two months, because at this age a baby's developing ability to focus and use her two eyes together would allow some cues to depth to be used for the first time.

At six months, babies do not crawl on to the 'cliff', so they show not only that they can see depth quite well, but also that they have had enough experience to exhibit fear of falling.

Here's looking at you!

By three months, a baby may not yet have gained motor control over her arms and legs, but she can control where she looks. This is an important step in development. Growing maturity of the visual motor system means that she has more control over where she looks, what she looks at and for how long. This has important implications for her developmental progress. The baby is in charge of her own visual learning channel, and what a baby most likes to look at is her caregivers.

Gaze is one of the most important attachment behaviours. Through a baby's control of gaze she can engage in social interactions with a caregiver. She can initiate such interactions – catch her caregiver's eye – and also end them through looking away. This continues the social bonding process in an important way, at a time when the baby is still unable actively to seek out contact by touch because she cannot yet move towards her caregivers.

In a study of mother and baby interactions, Kaye (1982) focused on the amount of time babies spent gazing at their mothers and noticed how this changed as the babies developed. It was found that, at six weeks of age, a baby spent fifty-five per cent of her time looking at her mother's face and that this dropped to thirty-six per cent of her time at thirteen weeks. At twenty-six weeks she spent twenty-nine per cent of her time gazing at her mother's face. A baby seems to be less interested in her mother's face as she gets older.

The study also showed, however, that, as she got older, a baby responded more to her mother. The six-week-old baby might gaze at her mother but she did not react very much. Any reactions tended to be in response to a particular behaviour on the part of the mother. By thirteen weeks, a baby responds more to her mother, returning a mother's greetings and smiles, and she initiates some of the interactions. By twenty-six weeks, a baby comes out with as many spontaneous greetings as her mother. In a short space of time, a baby has learned some of the rules of social engagement and greeting.

What's in a look?

Mothers and young babies spend an extraordinary amount of time just gazing at each other. In particular, mothers hold a much longer length of gaze with young babies than they ever do with either other adults or older children. This is less for the mother to learn her baby's features than to allow the baby to learn hers.

As well as holding extraordinarily long gazes, mothers also use more exaggerated expressions when looking at their babies. They tend to change their expressions more slowly and deliberately, and hold them for a longer length of time. This helps a baby to learn a particular face – it remains the same face through a great variety of transformations resulting from changed expressions.

In normal adult-to-adult communication, facial expressions change with great speed and

Mutual gazing is a very important attachment behaviour. The face-to-face interaction that this baby is having with a caregiver helps learning about communication. Such interactions can be maintained during games and in conversation.

show a wide range of subtle adjustments, which are confusing for a baby who is learning its form. The kind of slowing down of change and simplification of expression used by a caregiver helps a baby to learn not only to recognize a face but also to read faces. As adults we can read very subtle changes in expression on the faces of others; it's an important part of how we communicate. So babies need to start learning to decode such face messages from a very early age.

Learning of faces

At one month, when looking at faces, a baby tends to scan the boundaries. She is most interested in the edges of high contrast. At two months, a baby pays attention to particular features inside the face – eyes are a particular feature that she finds fascinating. By three months, a baby is beginning to have some idea of what a face is. She can differentiate a frowning and a smiling face, and prefers a smiling one. She can also recognize a photograph of her mother's face, and prefers to look at a photograph of her mother rather than one of a stranger.

By about five or six months, a baby can see a face as a whole rather than scanning the individual features. This helps her to discriminate between different faces. She can also quickly recognize whether a face is familiar. After six months, a baby has a good memory for the faces of particular individuals, which means that she must have developed some kind of stable representation of those faces.

LANGUAGE DEVELOPMENT

Baby talk

Babies like to listen to as well as look at their caregivers. From birth they seem to prefer speech sounds to other sounds, in particular listening to the sound of their mother's voice.

The primary aim of speech is communication, so in everyday life people adjust their speech to fit the audience. When adults talk to babies these adjustments to speech are very noticeable. They talk 'baby talk'. This kind of speech can sometimes be viewed with a certain degree of embarrassment or mockery by other adults, but it shouldn't be. It has features that make it an ideal language-learning environment for babies. Studies have shown that babies pay markedly more attention to adult speech directed towards them than to speech directed towards other adults. They seem to be especially sensitive to infant-directed speech. Babies prefer baby talk to 'normal' speech.

What are the differences between the two? What acoustic properties does baby talk have that are so attractive to babies?

When adults talk to young babies, typically they raise the pitch of their voices. We know that babies prefer higher sounds, in general, such as bells (which makes rattles with bells particularly appealing as first toys). They prefer higher-pitched voices, and pay more attention to high-pitched speech sounds.

Adults also elongate vowels when talking to babies making the typical 'ooooh!' and 'aaaaaah!' type sounds. They use lots of repetitions, repeating the same sound patterns, words or phrases over and over again. They speak more slowly and more rhythmically. As well as higher pitch, they typically use a broader pitch range with greater contrasts. This kind of simplified and exaggerated speech is similar to the simplified and exaggerated facial expressions that mothers tend to use with their babies.

Does baby talk help?

The special features of baby talk do seem to help a baby's language development. If you have to try to get meaning from a very complicated pattern, then anything that simplifies that pattern must help. Speech directed towards a baby by both its context and its own intrinsic features helps to gain a baby's attention. It also helps to focus that attention. The features of baby talk make for great contrast and coherence and these help the baby tune into the important features of speech long before she can extract meaning from the actual words used.

It has been suggested that babies have an inborn predisposition to tune into features of speech sounds, but undoubtedly experience of speech plays an important role in language development. Baby talk and early conversations provide the ideal contexts for learning about language. The more a caregiver talks directly to a baby, the more opportunity she has to extract information and the richer her learning environment.

Making sounds

As well as crying, a baby can produce a range of different sounds from very early on. These are important, not just as signals and social behaviours in interactions with caregivers, but also as part of what the baby herself can hear and learn from. She can listen to her own sounds and match up what she hears with how she moves her mouth and tongue and lips to produce them.

Under one month, the sounds produced by a baby tend to come directly from her particular physiological state. From one month, however, she may start to coo. These cooing noises arise out of interactions and signify pleasure – a bit like an audible smile. Between about six weeks and three months, babies make laughs, gurgles, squeals, and a variety of long drawn-out vowel sounds. She can use the muscles at the back of her mouth to make sounds through constriction. From three months on, she can produce a wider range of more speech-like sounds, including consonant sounds such as 'ka' or 'ga'. This reflects the baby's experience of listening to the language sounds around her. The sounds that a baby produces are usually restricted to those sounds that she hears most around her.

Babbling

By about six months, a baby may start babbling. This is repetition of strings of consonant–vowel combinations. She comes out with consonants and vowel strings and syllables such as 'ba' and 'da', either singly or in combinations, and repeats the sounds playfully. Babies babble to themselves and to others. The start of babbling shows the increasing maturity of a baby's vocal tract and mouth. It also shows the development of her fine motor skills and co-ordination in the control of her mouth, tongue and lips. The earliest vowel sounds are those that a baby makes at the back of her mouth. Then she can make vowel sounds produced at the front. A baby's earliest consonant sounds tend to be produced at the front of the mouth and then later on at the back of the mouth. It has been suggested that babbling is closely tied to the maturation of the brain, and later it becomes more speech-like as it takes on some of the intonation patterns of the speech that the baby hears around her. The repetitions develop patterns and at times seem to imitate adult vocalizations.

Communication

Babies attend to specific aspects of linguistic information; they like playing with linguistic elements. What is of primary importance is, however, communication. A baby gradually learns to produce sounds and to understand the meaning and grammar of utterances, but these linguistic skills develop as part of her growing ability to communicate. Her ability to communicate also encompasses understanding and being able to express herself with gestures, facial expressions and body movements. Acquiring language reflects not only a baby's biological endowment (ability to hear and produce vocalizations) and cognitive development but, just as importantly, it reflects a baby's growing social development. Babies learn language very much in a social context. If babies do not interact, or are not exposed to verbal interactions, then their learning is much impaired. This was seen in the language of a child of deaf parents whose primary exposure to spoken language was television. Her language skills did not develop despite the fact that, through television, she heard a lot of speech and both saw and heard conversations between adults.

Responding to talk

From very early on babies seem to learn some aspects of communication long before they can either understand or produce language. This learning about the patterning of communicative interactions between people is in fact a very important framework for all language learning.

Even very young babies, in the first few weeks after birth, have been observed to make small movements of their bodies and arms in response to being spoken to. They orientate themselves in a way that synchronizes with the pattern of the spoken words. These tiny movements and orientations of the body are very interesting because they seem to mirror what psychologists have noticed as occurring among adults.

When two speakers hold a conversation there are patterns of pauses and movements of head and body, as well as adjustments of gazing and looking away. Normally, we are unaware of this kind of meshing or choreography of conversations, but this does not mean that they are not important. If there is some disfunctioning of this ability, we are aware that something is wrong or lacking. This may in part explain how speakers of different languages often feel a lack of communication, apart from the purely linguistic elements of such dialogue. They have learned different conversation 'patterns'.

Even in the first few months of life, babies show a sensitivity to voices and speech which is expressed through their body movements. This shows a kind of early predisposition towards communication – an early responsiveness.

Early conversations

Observation studies have shown how mothers build on this responsiveness to hold 'conversations' with babies long before their babies are capable of understanding content or making any meaningful contribution. Mothers pace their interactions as if the babies are making a reply to the utterances. They interpret any noise or movement *as if it were a meaningful contribution* to an ongoing conversation. This imputing of some kind of intentional communication on behalf of the baby seems to be very important in the development of communication and later language skills. It is the ideal way for babies to learn the rules of how to communicate, long before there is any consideration of what it is they are trying to tell us.

Typically a mother starts by gaining attention in close face-to-face interaction. She then says something to her baby and pauses just long enough for the baby to contribute her turn in the conversation. Sometimes, the mother puts in the baby's contribution herself, before then taking her own turn again in the conversation.

In this way, a baby learns many features of person-to-person communication at a very early stage. She learns the idea of gaining attention before you say anything, of taking turns in speaking and then of listening. She learns the timing of these shifts in roles and the synchronization of eye gaze, utterance, facial expression and orientation of the body. All these features form the crucial underpinning of communication. Learning these rules of conversation is facilitated by these early one-to-one conversations between a baby and her caregiver.

Early games for two

These early conversations between caregiver and baby are part of a repertoire of early one-to-one interactions and games which babies enjoy so much at this stage. Play for a baby at this age means interacting with those people around her – people are her favourite playthings and early games provide a forum for early learning through play.

Babies start to enjoy small ritual games of repeated interaction sequences. They enjoy the social interactions and the sensations of, for example, being tickled or bounced up and down. They like it when one thing makes another happen and get pleasure out of seeing the pattern of such associations. They enjoy repetitions and soon learn to predict the sequences of simple games. Anticipation of a pleasurable outcome gives a baby great enjoyment and, at the same time, a baby is developing her cognitive and communicative skills through such games.

Most families develop their own personal stock of such games. What one baby finds vastly amusing may not work well with another. Individual games tend to grow and be modified with a baby's developing skills, as she tends to take a bigger and bigger part in the proceedings. Most games share the common features of starting from where the baby is at in terms of development and interest. They use the baby's involvement, interest and enjoyment as feedback to repeat or modify or abandon a game. The games are short and repetitive, and form an easily anticipated sequence of events leading to a pleasurable outcome. This repeated sequence of actions and repetitive language means that a baby soon recognizes the meaning of the game and can anticipate the playful outcome. The best games are ones that actually start from one of the baby's own behaviours and build up a ritual interaction sequence around this, which is why tickling games are so good. They start from a baby's own response to a stimulus and create a context within which a baby enjoys learning to anticipate some pleasurable happening.

Babies especially enjoy games that go through a predictable sequence leading to an enjoyable climax event. Many babies, for example, enjoy a pretend sneeze sequence. There is a build-up of tension as the caregiver says 'Ah! Ah! Ah!'. This is followed by a release of tension as the caregiver says 'Ah-choo!' and pretends to sneeze. The sequence ends in laughter, cuddles and tickles. Other varieties of games that babies enjoy include the 'Here it comes' type. A caregiver's hand wiggles fingers to get attention and then approaches closer and closer in stages as he counts one–two–three, then ends with a tickle. Numerous variations of this can be played using a soft toy in 'Here comes Teddy', or a hand puppet or even a caregiver's head to loom close to the baby after a short sequence of predictable steps, all accompanied by some repetition of

Babies get pleasure out of the pattern of contingencies. This baby is enjoying a tickling game with his mother, and will soon learn to anticipate sequences of actions.

either spoken or sung phrases. A baby enjoys these event sequences and very soon learns to anticipate what is going to happen. Games can then become more complex and involve story lines. There are many early games that generations of parents have played with their babies and which babies enjoy tremendously. For example:

> *Round and round the garden like a teddy bear.*
> *One step, two steps, then . . . tickle you under there.*

Here, the game starts with a circle drawn on a baby's palm before the adult's fingers step up the baby's arm to end in an armpit tickle. With 'This little piggy' the adult counts off a baby's toes one by one before again ending in a tickle. For both of these, the rhyme and repetitive nature of the language help to underpin the pattern of events and the sequence of what happens. All this makes it easier for a baby to learn to anticipate what is going to happen, and also to pick up some understanding of language and meaning from the same words occurring again and again in exactly the same context:

> *This little piggy went to market*
> *This little piggy stayed at home*
> *This little piggy had roast beef*
> *And this little piggy had none,*
> *And this little piggy cried 'wee wee wee'*
> *all the way home.*

More boisterous games suitable for perhaps slightly older babies include pretend falling games or bouncing games such as 'This is the way the farmer rides', in which a baby is bounced on an adult's knee in a variety of different ways. This last game can be tailored to individual babies and individual families. There is no reason why you cannot make up your own script to match a variety of different kinds of bouncing movements.

With something like 'All clap hands together' the game can begin with an action that the baby is not yet able to do. The caregiver acts as if the baby can, however. A caregiver uses his hands to make the baby clap hers together. At first she enjoys the sensation of movement and the touch of a caregiver's hands on hers, but soon she starts to enjoy the association of the clapping sounds with her own actions, especially if they are accompanied with perhaps a little clapping song from the caregiver. (Don't worry – babies are the best kind of an audience for a singer to have. They appreciate the song no matter what abilities the singer really has.) This is a game that, like others, develops and grows as a baby's abilities grow. In a surprisingly short time you might find that you don't have to manipulate the baby's own hands, as she starts to try and bring her own hands together. Later on, as the baby gets older the same game can be the stimulus for her own independent clapping of hands. Even before she is capable of doing this under her own steam, she shows by her attempts that she knows the sequence of what is meant to happen. When you clap your hands she becomes excited and makes rudimentary arm waving, and then does so when you start to sing the song. This can grow into games like 'Pat-a-cake', for example:

> *Pat-a-cake, pat-a-cake, baker's man,*
> *Bake me a cake as fast as you can.*
> *Pat it and prick it and mark it with B.*
> *And there will be plenty for baby and me.*

All these basic games can evolve to incorporate a baby's growing abilities and repertoire of behaviours. The important thing is for caregivers to be sensitive to the baby's needs and abilities in such playful interactions. They need to match their behaviour with a baby's ability to attend and join in. Initially, a baby can only signal that she has had enough by looking away. It is important for caregivers to treat this gaze aversion as finishing an interaction, until the baby wants to start it up again by engaging the caregiver's eye once more. Later on, as her abilities grow, a caregiver must let a baby take a bigger part in playing the games. She may want to initiate them, for example, or try and tickle the caregiver back again.

It is maybe stating the obvious, but the main reason babies like these social games is that they are sharing an enjoyable event with some- one close to them. It is the positive emotions that are important rather than the games themselves. It is very important to show, by the tone of voice and facial expression, how much you are enjoying the interaction with a baby in order to get back similar positive emotions.

Benefits for language development

There is a link between the style of mother–child interactions and a child's later size of vocabulary. Children of mothers who engage in more one-to-one conversations and early games when the babies are young tend to have more advanced language at the age of two. Across cultures, Italian babies, who play more ritual games than American babies, tend to be more advanced in their speech. On the other hand, other cultures have completely different child-rearing practices. Among some Indian tribes, there is much less face-to-face interaction during the first year of life, yet the infants of these tribes still learn how to carry on conversations with others and are able to communicate effectively.

It seems as if early face-to-face dialogues, turn-taking games and interactions may not be necessary for language learning to take place, but they can help children acquire language skills and acquire them earlier.

This baby is having a face-to-face interaction with her mother. Such early face-to-face dialogues and conversations help children acquire language skills.

CHAPTER THREE

THE OLDER BABY

six to twelve months

The non-stop explorer

In six short months of life, a baby has managed to establish himself as a member of the family. He is already a person woven into a social fabric of family and culture. He has changed in so many ways that he seems a different being from the helpless newborn of such a short time ago. His senses have developed so that to all intents and purposes they can be treated as functioning the same way as in adults. (Although this is not really true for a baby's eyesight which throughout the pre-school period does not have the same acuity as that of an adult in close focus. In contrast, their ability to see at distance is much better than that of most adults.)

This, together with increased motor control of limbs and the beginnings of an ability to change viewpoints by changing position, means that a baby has the skills needed to become a non-stop explorer of his environment. As he starts to develop the ability to move around, this environment becomes the whole wide world.

From six to twelve months, a baby is consumed with curiosity about everything. His curiosity extends also to testing the limits of his own motor skills and abilities. A caregiver has to try both to facilitate and to encourage that curiosity, but in a way that ensures the baby's well-being and safety, and finding this balance is not always easy. A balance has to suit both a baby's temperament and a caregiver's time and patience. Just as it is unhelpful to have unrealistic expectations of how a baby can behave at a particular stage in his development, it is also unhelpful to have unrealistic expectations of a caregiver's role. The primary role, at this stage as in all stages, is for a loving and responsive attitude towards a baby so that he has a secure sense of trust. A caregiver is an interested partner in a child's development and can have an important input and effects on the progress of that development – but remember that it is the baby's own development. He begins to have more and more control over his own learning as he develops. This is true for both what he learns and how he learns.

MOTOR DEVELOPMENT

During this period, a baby makes big developmental strides in both the gross movement skills (such as walking) and the fine movement skills (such as manual dexterity). From being a relatively helpless immobile baby, by the end of his first year of life he can move around under his own steam. He has the motor skills needed to explore the environment in a systematic and effective way. These developments occur in a regular sequence and at a similar rate for most babies and reflect, to a great extent, a baby's biological maturation. This does not mean, however, that a baby's experience and other environmental factors don't also play a role in the development of specific motor skills.

Sitting

A baby can sit up without support at this time. This requires fine tuning of balance and good muscle control for the small compensatory movements that keep a baby upright. Sitting isn't as easy as it looks. Initially a baby needs support under the arms and later some support at tummy level. Babies vary in their ability to sit unaided. By the time some babies manage it, they may already be able to move, and moving around is so much fun that a baby may not sit still very much at all, even though he can.

Other babies, by temperament, seem to enjoy sitting and watching the world from this new vantage point and, if provided with an adequate supply of reachable interesting objects, they sit quite happily either in prams or on rugs.

Getting mobile

Getting around under his own steam is a turning point for the baby - influencing cognitive and emotional development in many important ways. A baby not only gets a new and changing view of his surroundings, he can also interact much more directly with them. This feeds back into his own sense of agency and the way he can act on the world. The ways in which he interacts with a caregiver also undergo

some readjustments at this time. These have far-reaching effects on both how he understands the world and how he views his own position within that world.

Rolling

At about six months a baby can roll over from his front to his back. By seven to eight months he may also be able to roll from his back to his front and then he can start to move from one place to another without anyone's help. Just as they enjoyed kicking their legs for the pleasure in the sensation, so babies enjoy moving their bodies from place to place for the joy of the sensation. A baby can also be very determined in using all the skills at his disposal to reach something that has caught his attention, so when he sees something that he wants he makes an effort to reach it. By repeated rolling movements, it is amazing how much ground a baby can cover in pursuit of his objectives.

Crawling

At about nine months, a baby may start to crawl. The actual movement can vary, and some people differentiate this kind of locomotion into crawling and creeping. At first a baby may not be able to lift his tummy off

This baby is crawling towards something he wants. Crawling can be a very efficient way of covering surprisingly big distances in a short space of time.

the ground. He tends to drag himself around using his arms, so the motion is more of a 'self-haul'. Sometimes a baby moves like this but then finds out that he can use his toes as well to push against the ground and help him along. On other occasions, he is more successful at pushing against the ground than in pulling with his arms, so he may change to a kind of backward motion in which he pushes with his arms as a way of moving.

Later on he may get up on knees and arms in what is considered a proper crawl. Crawling can be a very fast and efficient way of covering large distances in a short space of time, as many caregivers soon come to realize. Even after they have taken their first full walking steps, many crawlers still prefer that form of locomotion if they have to get somewhere particularly attractive in a hurry.

Shuffling

Some babies do not, however, learn to crawl. Some shuffle around in an upright sitting position using their legs to propel themselves, others combine different kinds of locomotion such as rolling and shuffling, some develop their own idiosyncratic ways of moving.

This baby is being given a hand by another child to stand upright. Once a baby walks, and is then a 'toddler', he has reached a milestone in his physical development.

Walking

The sequence in which a baby acquires the ability to perform certain motor skills is fairly predictable, and these skills then build up towards the point at which a baby is able to walk. Walking unaided is a milestone in a baby's physical development – a turning point when parents see the child start to emerge from babyhood. When other aspects of a child's early history are forgotten, parents often remember exactly when a baby took his first steps. The sequence of pre-walking motor skills acquired by a baby includes the stages shown in the box.

There seems to be a natural progression in the development of motor skills leading up to walking, and this progression unfolds simply with biological maturation. Unless handicapped in some way, all children learn to walk usually at the end of their first year of life, but not all of them acquire these skills in the same or in any predictable sequence. Some, in fact, do not learn these particular skills at all and yet still go on to walk. Although biological maturation underpins the development of walking, there is also a very wide variation among 'normal' babies at the age when they first start to walk. This can vary from nine to eighteen months.

Why is there such a large variation?

SEQUENCE OF PRE-WALKING MOTOR SKILLS

❖ Sitting up without needing support

❖ Able to stand up by holding on to furniture

❖ Able to pull into a standing position

❖ Moving around holding on to furniture – using shuffling sideways steps

❖ Walking holding on to a caregiver's hand

Effects of environment

One thing that can vary is the different experiences in a baby's life which might accelerate or hinder motor development. For example, an extremely restricted environment with few opportunities to practise any movements might slow down the age at which a baby starts to move, or unstimulating surroundings might have a negative effect on a baby's curiosity, so that there is less motivation to explore his surroundings and become mobile. Certainly, some children brought up in deprived environments, for example, those of some orphanages in less developed countries or trouble spots in the world, showed an inability to walk even at two years of age. This slowed development was, however, found to be temporary.

Different child-rearing practices

Different societies and cultures regard different skills and accomplishments as being more or less valued and important. This is reflected in the way that different cultures encourage the development of those skills among their children. In African cultures babies are propped upright from an early age to encourage sitting. They are also encouraged to practise stepping and walking behaviour by being held upright. Their limbs are manipulated to encourage early walking. This reflects the higher value placed upon early walking and early sitting. African caregivers actively encourage these skills in their babies and it has been shown that African babies learn to walk on average two months earlier than American babies. Other cross-cultural studies have shown that Mexican babies lag behind American babies in locomotion, which could reflect differences in environment. For example, Mexican babies are not put down on the ground to play but are carried around, and they sleep in hammocks rather than in cots.

Among one tribe of Indians in Paraguay, a common finding was that infants didn't walk until about eighteen months of age. This was attributed to direct child-rearing practice, because mothers actively discouraged mobility. If a baby tried to crawl away he would be pulled back onto the mother's lap.

Yet, on the other hand, other restrictions of movements seem to have little effect on the onset of walking. For example, there is little difference between Navaho (American Indian) and other American babies in the onset of walking, despite the Navaho practice of swaddling their infants tightly which could be expected to have some impact on motor development. One early study of Hopi Indians investigated the effects of their child rearing on the baby's later motor development – specifically the onset of walking. The Hopi used cradling boards. A baby was not only swaddled tightly, but tied on to a board which completely restricted the baby's ability to move around. For the first three months, a baby spent almost all of his time in this position, even being nursed while tied to the cradling board. The Hopi used the boards for more than six months. When groups of Indians who used the cradling boards were compared with groups who did not, however, little or no difference was found in the age at which babies first started to walk (Dennis and Dennis, 1940).

The evidence from cross-cultural studies does therefore seem to be contradictory. On the whole, it seems as if some child-rearing practices can have effects on motor development, either to slow down or to speed up the acquisition of some skills, but they may not be long lasting.

Here I come: a baby's first steps towards the goal of reaching a pair of familiar hands. First attempts to walk unaided occur over a range of time, but are usually around the end of the first year.

Training of motor skills

Can motor development be speeded up by training? Studies have investigated the efficacy of direct training on the acquisition of motor skills. The most famous studies have used twins for comparison – one who received training and one who did not. This was to ensure that maturation was exactly the same for both the infants and that the only difference between the two was in the training. It was found that even

intensive training had only a slight effect. The untrained twin very quickly caught up with the trained one, so that the effort involved in intensive training did not seem worth while. Maturation seemed to be more important than practice or training (Gesell and Thomson, 1929)

Recently, however, this study has been criticized for the kind of activity that constituted training. It was suggested that the training did not work because it wasn't really useful for acquiring motor skills, for example, one of the motor skills trained was climbing stairs, in which the trained twin was initially simply lifted from one step to the next.

Ready to go

A baby starts to walk when he is ready to do so. His readiness is influenced by a variety of factors, some of which, like maturation, are very much to do with genetic factors over which he has no control. Other environmental factors concerned with child-rearing practice may have some influence, but the baseline is that a baby walks when he is ready to do so. His readiness is influenced as much by his own temperament as by any encouragement given by caregivers. The main thing is to respond positively to a baby whatever stage he is at, and whatever motor skills he possesses. Encouraging him in his efforts when he tries to do something is more important than imposing a timetable arranged according to a caregiver's expectations.

MANIPULATION SKILLS
Holding and letting go

At four months, if a baby is holding an object in his hand and you offer a second object he will drop the first one in order to take the second. By seven months, in the same situation, he can transfer the first object to his other hand before he takes hold of the second one.

At this stage he can hold onto small objects and gradually he develops the skilled pincer grip between finger and thumb; by about nine months he can use this grip to pick up very small objects such as a raisin or a grain of rice. At much the same time, he gains more fine control of his grip so that he can let go of things intentionally. Before this stage, objects get dropped, of course, but this is different. Now he can offer something to someone and actually give it to them. He can consciously relax and release his grip rather than just forget to hold on.

SOME PHYSICAL PLAY

AS YOU CAN see from this baby's expression, baby bouncers are fun. They love the sensation of movement, and touching bare feet on a variety of surfaces that give different touch sensations can be even more stimulating. Smooth lino, velvet, furry fabric or soft sand in a tray can all add a variety of different touch experiences for bouncing baby feet. Material that makes a noise, such as crumpled paper or a bowl of water to make a nice splashy sound, adds to the pleasure.

Push-along and pull-along toys are encouraging to babies who are starting to become mobile.

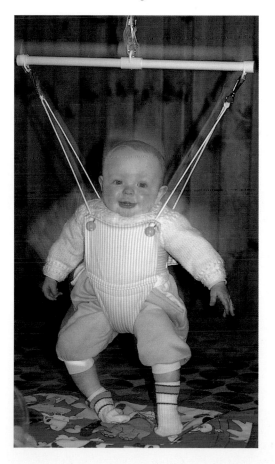

Exploring objects

As his fine movement skills develop a baby uses his hands to explore objects, as well as his mouth. Over time the amount of exploration by mouthing decreases and that by manipulation tends to increase.

He has better control of both finger and wrist movement so he can co-ordinate two objects such as a spoon and a box. He can bring together two hands that are both holding an object. He can bang the two together. Babies love to explore the nature of objects at this time and the fact that sometimes two together make a noise is a real bonus. Quick to make connect-ions between cause and effect, a baby makes endless experiments into the sound-making properties of objects!

EXPLORATORY PLAY

Babies love playing with small, easily held objects. They enjoy reaching out for, grasping, looking at, mouthing and touching things. Novelty is quite important, so a variety of interesting but safe objects (not necessarily toys) is a good idea. A baby enjoys playing with containers and the things that can go inside them and be taken out again. Rattles and other noise-making toys are also of great interest at this time. A baby tends to like things that can be pressed, squeezed, poked, prodded or otherwise acted upon, and that do something interesting in response. Babies enjoy wind-up musical toys and jack-in-the-boxes, but often they are unable to manipulate them by themselves early on so they need help from a caregiver. This can be frustrating for some babies who want to play with and explore things independently. Other babies enjoy the social interaction with caregivers that play with such toys entails.

He also enjoys knocking things over to see what happens. If a caregiver builds up a tower of bricks, the baby soon learns how to demolish it. After a bit, it is hard to get the baby to refrain from the demolition long enough to allow the building process. Building with blocks is a separate activity and one that develops later. It may need more encouragement and guidance from caregivers.

Reaching

A baby's ability to reach and grasp hold of things becomes refined during this time, as a result of both maturation and his experience of being

At this stage, babies love knocking things down. It is some time before they are interested in building the bricks up themselves. The social interaction engendered by such play is also important.

given objects to hold. Very young babies have a kind of reaching reflex, whereby they may reach and grasp for an object in their immediate surroundings. This movement is, however, a kind of undifferentiated whole in which the reach and the grasp are not separate but part of a single movement pattern. It is also pretty unsuccessful on the whole, babies tending to miss the object that they are trying to get.

At this stage, babies are developing and refining a mature reaching and grasping that is two separate behaviours. The baby only tries to grasp something once he has reached it successfully. He reaches using visual guidance which is confirmed by touch. He then gets feedback about the position and movement of his fingers in relation to both the object and his own body sense. This is a qualitatively different kind of reaching from earlier behaviour. Now there is a delay, while the baby confirms via sensory feedback that he is on target, before his fingers grasp hold of the desired object. This more mature kind of reaching is much more successful. The baby is much more likely to hit his target and thus get feedback about his own performance and the reward which motivates him to try the same behaviour again.

A baby learns to refine and improve this behaviour by such experience. Having lots of opportunities to reach for and grasp small

Objects that make a sound provide a lot of stimulus for babies. This baby is enjoying exploring the sound-making properties of two objects.

objects is very important for the development of this skill. Rattles and other toys that are safe, easy to hold and interesting to explore come into their own at this stage. Variety is very important because it is often the novelty of an object that is its chief attraction for a baby. It does not have to be an expensive toy. Any object that fits the criteria of safety and size – not too small for a child to swallow, but not too large for a child to hold – may be used. Empty containers, cotton reels, etc. can become instant toys either on their own or grouped together by being threaded onto strings.

DEVELOPMENT OF THINKING
Learning to understand the world

Babies have different preferred styles when it comes to interacting with the world. Some like to touch while others like to look, but all babies at this age do tend to stare a lot. They use their eyes to scrutinize people and things in order to get information. Sometimes such intense scrutiny can be unnerving for those at the receiving end, as it seems to be done with such serious intent. This is because it is a serious business. Babies are in the process of transforming the unknown into the known.

At this stage, they still have very different ways of perceiving the world and understanding what they see. For example, young babies do not have the same idea about objects as adults. To begin with, for a baby, an object ceases to exist if it is not immediately perceived. If he is shown an object and then a caregiver puts that object inside a container, a baby acts as if it has disappeared. He doesn't seem to understand that the object is still there but just inside the container. This idea of *object permanence* develops only gradually during the baby's first year.

Person permanence

Young babies don't as yet have the idea that a single object can appear in many places. An object in a different place becomes a different object. This can be demonstrated with babies who were shown multiple images of their mother in reflections. They could see three mothers at the same time. Babies under five months old were not distressed by this at all – it seemed perfectly normal for them. They smiled and interacted with their three reflected mothers. However, for babies over five months it was a different story. When they saw three mothers they were very disturbed.

It is fascinating to watch a baby become absorbed in something. New things provide opportunities for such exploration and attention.

The explanation is that, by the second half of his first year, a baby has worked out that he has only one mother. She might appear in many different places, but she stays the one person. He has developed a kind of *person permanence* if you like. Therefore, something that violates his sense of what is correct is quite upsetting. The three reflected mother images went against what he knows to be true – that he has only one mother – and he was justifiably disturbed.

Object permanence

The idea that an object has the same kind of permanence develops gradually over the second half of a baby's first year. To begin with, for a baby, out of sight does seem to mean out of mind. Only over time does a baby get the idea that an object continues to exist even if he cannot see it and this happens in stages.

When a toy is hidden underneath a cloth, it has ceased to exist for a baby. He can find the toy if part of it is sticking out. Between eight and twelve months, he learns-to find the toy even when it is completely hidden under the cloth. A little later he will show surprise if the cloth is pulled away and there is no toy.

What is going on with the younger babies? What do we mean exactly when we say 'out of sight out of mind'?

One explanation could be that the baby has such a short memory that he quickly forgets about the toy. As he develops, his memory improves so that he can remember about the

By putting things in and out of containers, this baby is developing a •
concept of object permanence.

Gestures

A child employs a variety of gestures to help him communicate at this period. For example, by about nine to twelve months he may shake his head when he doesn't want something or to signal that he has had enough to eat. He waves his hand to say 'bye-bye' when someone leaves. He may nod his head to signal that he wants something in response to a question and stretch out his arms to signal that he wants to be picked up. (Although to begin with this normally doesn't imply a request so much as the baby anticipating what for him is the usual sequence of events.) Giving, showing and pointing are used as little communicative acts. A baby may also open and close his palm, as a kind of ritualization of the grasping act, into a grasping gesture with the meaning 'give that thing to me'.

Towards the end of his first year, a baby may use a pointing gesture to draw a person's attention to something. This develops from a simple imitation of adult pointing in a similar context to a gesture with a range of meaning from 'Look at that!' to 'I want that!'.

Understanding a caregiver

Non-verbal signals

In the second half of a baby's first year, he becomes skilled at getting information through reading a caregiver's facial expression. He uses this especially in situations in which he is unsure of what to do, or how to react. For example, in the visual cliff experiment to test a baby's depth perception, a baby often looks over to his caregiver's face to find out if it is safe to crawl across the glass or not. He uses the cues that his caregiver gives – either positive or negative – and acts appropriately. This is called social referencing and makes a great deal of sense. It is something that we all do even as adults. In a situation in which we are unsure of how to act, we take our cues by looking at other people and how they seem to be reacting.

A baby of about eight months can also get information from the direction of a caregiver's gaze and then later from a caregiver's pointing. For a young baby, a pointing gesture has little meaning. He is likely to look at the caregiver's finger rather than the object.

This toddler is pointing something out to his mother. From the end of his first year, pointing gestures are used for drawing a person's attention to something.

The ability to understand the meaning of a point develops gradually and seems to grow from the joint focusing of attention between a caregiver and a baby which is such an important part of early interactions and games. A point may grow from the touching gestures a caregiver uses first to get a baby's attention on an object. Pointing develops as a kind of long distance touch and this is how it comes to be understood by a baby.

Understanding what is said

Whenever they are spoken to, babies try hard to understand the intent and the meaning of what is being said. Non-verbal clues to meaning, such as facial expression and gesture, help a baby to understand. He also tries to extract understanding from the context of any particular communicative utterance. This is where every-day routines help in language learning. When he is being changed, for example, the same objects are produced in the same order and the same sequence of actions is performed. They provide a consistent regular context within which a baby hears certain words and phrases repeated. Soon he learns the meaning of the words through the context in which they regularly occur. The first words a baby learns are those associated with his day-to-day routines. It is helpful, therefore, to introduce the same naming of objects and repeated discussion of what you are doing into daily routines because these provide the best situation for a baby to understand the meaning of the language you use.

A baby comes to understand those words that he hears most frequently and that occur in association with particular events, happenings or people. So he tends to recognize his own name, and the names of those around him whom he sees most often, such as siblings or pets or 'mummy' and 'daddy'. He understands the meaning of 'bye-bye', in the first instance when it is accompanied by a waving gesture and then without such a gesture, just the words. He understands the meaning of 'no' as a prohibition on whatever he is doing at the time.

SOCIAL AND EMOTIONAL DEVELOPMENT
Social world

It is important to remember that a baby's world is primarily a social world. He may be a non-stop explorer at this age, but what interests him most are people and his relationships within a social world. He is driven to learn through exploration, but what he wants to explore most of all is how to interact with others. When we talk about exploration of objects, it is easy to imagine a baby as some kind of coolly detached scientist from the planet **womb**, but it is important to remember that his first drive is to learn to be a functioning member of society. It is this that underpins and provides the meaningful context for all a baby's cognitive and language development. It is very often within an extremely social context that a baby first exhibits a kind of developed thinking ability, which he can use only much later in wider, more context-free situations. For example, the early teasing behaviour of a baby shows the kind of sophist-icated thinking that he cannot use in other areas until he is much older. Similarly, the thinking skills underpinning the ability to pretend are not transferred to his ability to problem solve until much later.

These thinking skills that underpin teasing and pretend play develop within a social context of playful interaction with caregivers. Caregivers first play pretend games with babies at a very early age. Babies learn directly by copying routines that only later do they understand. It is through such play that babies develop their thinking skills.

Emotional development

We talk about a baby's growing ability to communicate at this time but, of course, a baby has been able to communicate effectively with his caregiver from birth, on a directly emotional level through gaze, movement, touch and voice.

What is developing is the ability to communicate in a more public form, transferable to a wider audience. By this we usually mean the development of a particular system of language. This can be seen as a process of loss as well as of gain. As language comes to dominate the way in which we express ourselves, we gradually lose our access to the direct emotional communication and expression that a baby enjoys within his first close relationship.

During the second half of his first year, a baby's relationship with those he feels closest to undergoes some changes. Obviously, with an ability to move a baby can actively seek out his caregiver. For the first time he has the power to regulate his own closeness or distance from his caregiver and very often he chooses to spend his time in close proximity. This is especially true if he is in a situation in which he feels unsure of himself. Often, in a new place a baby at this stage sticks close to his caregiver until he feels happy enough to explore. Often he uses glances to maintain contact when he moves off on his own.

Stranger anxiety

At about eight months, a baby may for the first time show some wariness of people whom he does not know. Up until then, a baby has usually shown himself to be quite happy to interact with anybody. Indeed, in the first few months, a baby shows a kind of indiscriminate sociability and it is only over time that certain people close to him become singled out for special affection. Up until then he does not show any preferences but smiles and interacts with anyone.

At eight months, however, a baby's growing attachment to one or more caregiver(s) reaches the stage that he not only prefers them, but may also show anxiety with unfamiliar people.

It is perhaps good for working parents to bear this in mind when planning child care plans and schedules. It may be easier to introduce new caregivers into a baby's life before

This baby looks distressed – his mother/caregiver has probably just left him. Babies usually first start to show some wariness of people they don't know and some distress if their mothers leave them at around eight months.

he develops this kind of distinction between familiar and unfamiliar people.

Not all babies show this kind of stranger anxiety, however. With some it amounts to a close scrutiny of an unfamiliar person, in the same way as they observe any novel object in their environment. The scrutiny may look like wariness, but is not accompanied by any particularly negative emotions.

Some people have attributed stranger wariness to a baby's cognitive development, rather than to any emotional changes occurring at this time. As he has a growing ability to remember, he can recall whether he has come across someone before and is therefore able to make a discrimination between familiar and unfamiliar which he was unable to do before.

CHAPTER FOUR

THE TODDLER

twelve to twenty-four months

At this stage a baby is a powerhouse of activity. She is developing new skills and abilities so fast that it sometimes seems hard to keep up. The helplessness of early infancy has been left behind and she is very much an active explorer of her environment. She has an insatiable curiosity to explore everything, including her own developing abilities. She spends a lot of time practising recently acquired skills until she achieves mastery. And at the same time she has a drive to seek out new challenges and try out new skills.

MOTOR DEVELOPMENT

As she still has babyish proportions – with a trunk that is still a bit top heavy – to begin with, she walks with the toddling gait that gives a name to this age. She uses her arms for balance to start with and may have to watch her feet still. All this makes her seem a bit ungainly and clumsy. In just a short time, however, she makes great development in the co-ordination of her movements. Her balance improves and she becomes more secure and confident. Gradually, her walking action becomes smoother. Her steps become less tottery and irregular. After all she is getting a lot of practice!

Running and jumping

By the end of her second year, a toddler starts to jump. Initially, this is more a kind of extension of reaching which happens to involve a foot or feet briefly losing contact with the ground.

During her second year, she starts to run, although to begin with this is more like a hurried walk than a true run. When she does run she has difficulty in coming to a halt.

At this stage, she is very interested in play that practises her motor skills. She seems to take some delight in a growing mastery of movements both for their own sake and for the extended access they allow her for exploration.

Climbing

Her ability to climb develops rapidly at this time. From an ability to get up to about six inches off the ground, she can now climb up a foot or more. Some babies are adept at climbing long before they can walk. Some toddlers enjoy the different perspective a high viewpoint gives them. They become very good at putting together sequences of climbing movements and can end up very high indeed.

Steps and stairs are endlessly fascinating and children learn to go up them very early on. Coming down stairs is a different skill and unfortunately develops a bit later than ascending. Vigilance is the watchword for caregivers. Some people prefer to use gates to keep stairs toddler proof. Others prefer to allow their children to use stairs from early on, but teach a specific rule which they are very firm about the child obeying, for example, the child has to come down stairs by bumping down on her bottom first. It depends very much on the individual child and caregiver, as the people who have to work out a balance of safety, toddler independence and caregiver stress level to suit everyone concerned.

Interest in wheels

At this stage push-along and pull-along toys are very useful for a toddler to practise her motor skills. Toddlers seem to have a fascination with any toy that has wheels. As children tend, at this stage, to tumble over and fall a lot anyway, toys should be chosen carefully so as to help rather than hinder their safe progress. Some push-along toys are too light, for example, especially for beginner walkers, and don't have a low enough centre of gravity to stop it tipping over when a baby leans too heavily.

Playgrounds

A baby starts to enjoy lots of different kinds of movement now, so playgrounds, with swings, roundabouts, slides, and sit and ride toys may exert some fascination. It often seems as if the moment a baby has mastered upright locomotion, then she is immediately on the look-out for better thrills. This is just a symptom of her insatiable curiosity and strong desire to try out and master new experiences. This is often a very trying time given the gap between what a toddler would like to be able to do and realistic considerations of her abilities, and a caregiver has to balance everything with safety in mind. A lot of playground equipment is just not safe for toddlers, and the rest is only

Once toddlers are becoming mobile, push-along toys stimulate movement and can give confidence to beginner walkers. Make sure that the toys are suitable, not too light, for example.

Toddlers love practising their motor skills. Here one practises the fine movement skills involved in manipulating the pieces of a jigsaw puzzle.

safe if a toddler is closely supervised at all times. A lot of friction can occur between toddler and caregiver as a result of this mismatch between necessary supervision of her motor activity and the toddler's growing sense of her own ability and desire to exercise it.

Motor skill play

Toddlers take a great delight in mastering different motor skills and spend a lot of time in the kind of play that amounts to practise of those skills. This is something they do anyway, but it is a good idea to encourage it and perhaps widen their experiences. A lot of cognitive development is based on motor skills. Motor, cognitive and social skills are all intertwined in a child's developmental progress. Before she can do a jigsaw puzzle, a child must acquire not only the cognitive skills for matching the pictures and understanding how to solve the puzzle, but also the motor skills for manipulating the pieces correctly to fit. So it is a good idea to encourage play that practises such twisting wrist movements. Screwing and unscrewing jars and screws, hammering and pulling out pegs, and general manipulative play with objects all help a toddler's development.

Walking up and down slopes is a new experience for beginning walkers and they often enjoy the sensation. They learn about balance and muscle control. A toddler enjoys walking on different surfaces and textures in bare feet and all this again helps to improve her motor control. She gets a lot out of physical play in a safe environment with lots of cushions around to make tumbling fun rather than painful.

Lifting, fetching, carrying

Toddlers enjoy carrying things around from place to place and this is good practice for

A posting box is very good for helping in the development of fine motor skills. This child is learning about shape and colour through play with a posting box, together with her caregiver. The caregiver needs to talk about what the child is doing so she can get the full benefit.

hand–eye co-ordination. Lifting and manipulating objects and containers can provide lots of amusement and, at the same time, she is learning about the properties of those objects as well as practising her fine motor skills. Often household objects, such as the contents of kitchen cupboards, are more interesting than toys for a toddler. She is learning about the feel of different size and weight objects in her hands as she lifts them around and also co-ordinates information from a variety of sources. Household objects, pots and pans, packaging and tins

Toddlers have an extraordinary love of household items and want to help with household tasks. Although this makes the tasks much slower for mothers, they can often provide an opportunity for toddlers to count objects, to sort and match things, and to talk about colours.

of food give her more variety of experiences than any toys, so it is worthwhile putting up with the mess and inconvenience. It is also a good idea to decide beforehand what you will not allow her access to. Child-proof cupboard locks can then be fitted where appropriate.

A toddler enjoys playing with a ball at this stage, and various different size and weight balls give her different experiences. She likes learning about the motion of objects along surfaces and through space and water. Ball play is good for development and refinement of hand–eye co-ordination and fine motor control of wrist and fingers. She gradually learns the techniques of aiming and letting go as her ball throwing develops. To begin with catching happens only as a fortuitous circumstance when an adult thrower lands the ball in her lap or cupped hands. This is more of a passive receiving than catching. It takes quite a long time before a child can attempt to catch even an accurately thrown ball.

SOCIAL DEVELOPMENT

Separation anxiety

At this stage, a toddler continues in her close relationship with one or more of her caregivers – termed 'attachment'. This relationship continues to grow and develop. At this stage, a toddler has also formed relationships with other significant adults and any siblings. Through the development of a sense of trust within such relationships, a toddler has the confidence to explore her surroundings. She looks to a caregiver for reassurance whenever she feels insecure or unhappy.

Separation anxiety occurs when a toddler clings to her caregiver and does not like it when he or she leaves. She may become very upset and, when the caregiver returns, clings onto him or her like a limpet. This kind of behaviour first occurs around nine months of age, but often seems to get worse at the age of one to two.

Separation anxiety is related to a baby's growing concept of person permanence. She has to realize that she has a mother who continues to exist somewhere else before she can get upset about her leaving. This would perhaps explain why it occurs first at about the time that this kind of concept develops. It has also been suggested that such anxiety is also related, however, to a baby's communications development. By this stage, a baby and her caregiver have already built up a very good system of communicating, based on gestures, movement, vocalisations and an ability for each to interpret these signs in the other. So when, for example, a caregiver goes off somewhere, the baby is left feeling not only that she cannot understand the people she is left with, but also that nobody can understand her. No wonder she is upset.

Fear of strangers

Sometimes it is during the early half of her second year that a toddler may experience acute fear of strangers. Although this occurs with younger babies (usually around eight months), often it does not have the same emotional strength as now. At the same time, a toddler has a competing drive of curiosity: she is very interested in everything around her and especially people. Individual toddlers show large variations resulting from different experiences and temperaments. Some toddlers do go through an anxious phase, whereas others may show no fear of strangers.

Interest in other babies

Babies in the first half of their second year are very interested in other babies. In one study, it was shown that when pairs of mothers and babies played together, although the babies touched their own mothers more, they spent more time looking at the other babies.

Toddlers need a caregiver for reassurance, but their interest is definitely directed to the outside world of new, interesting people and

Other babies are often more interesting to babies and toddlers than adults, although they often spend more time looking at other babies than touching them.

The social interactions of toddlers often lead to tears, although any conflict is not intentional. These are skills that they learn through having the opportunity to interact.

things. Other babies or children are even more interesting than adults, although at mother and toddler groups, for example, they cannot, at this stage, really play together very much at all. The social skills of playing together vary with an individual's experience. If a toddler has older siblings then she is more able to play with others because she has more experience of how to behave. Often it seems that toddlers would like to interact more with others of the same age, but lack the social skills to do so successfully.

One strategy, such as joint focus in which a toddler focuses attention on an object that the other child is paying attention to, tends to backfire on the fledgling socialite. As social behaviour, joint attention works marvellously with a caregiver. The caregiver usually shares the object, names it, talks about it and may use it to start a game. As interactive behaviour with another toddler, it is not such a good idea, however. It is not seen as joint attention so much as toy snatching. Grabbing another's toy may be done with no malicious intent, but the effect is usually either to curtail a social interaction or to result in a negative one.

Toddlers are not unaware of the distress of other children. They seem to register the other child's hurt and may even become distressed themselves. Often they might try to help, but do so in an inappropriate manner, for example, by offering a toy to a toddler who is crying because she has fallen.

At this stage, she has a desire to interact but is not very skilled at managing social interactions with children of the same age. At toddler groups, caregivers have to spend a lot of time monitoring or intervening in any social encounters between babies. A toddler has to learn the rules of social interaction. Initially, the toddler is unable to make the distinction between herself and others. She cannot really understand what it is either to share or to take turns and has no real notion of ownership. She does not have the concept that some things belong to her and other things belong to others.

Development of autonomy

At the same time as fostering the close relationship with her caregiver, a toddler starts to want some independence at this stage. This is the start of a natural process whereby a child gradually replaces the almost symbiotic relationship she has with the caregiver by a more mature relationship of mutual respect and trust.

At this stage a toddler is testing out her newfound notions that she is an individual who has the power and ability to act on the world. This involves some idea of her sense of who she is, what she can do and also what she wants to do. This goes along with her growing sense of mastery of certain skills. Unfortunately, the competing drives towards independence and attachment can often make for strong emotions at this time. The conflict between safety and a toddler's abilities can lead to clashes between a caregiver and a toddler. These can lead to tantrums – unreasonable, angry behaviour by the child. The *terrible twos* is a phrase often used to describe the clashes that may occur. A

Terrible twos. A growing sense of autonomy in the child can lead to clashes at this time. Because he still has a limited ability to express his feelings verbally, this may lead to frustrations being expressed in temper tantrums.

toddler's developing sense of self and ideas of what she wants to do occurs at a time when she may have a limited ability to express her feelings in words, and this can lead to those strong feelings being expressed in tantrum behaviour. This does not explain them away, of course. A caregiver still has to cope with such behaviours, but it helps sometimes to understand that it is a phase that the child is going through, for particular developmental reasons.

One tactic to use to make the phase as short-lived as possible is to help her to learn to express herself in other less trying ways. Tantrums are usually sparked by particular situations and frustrations. Learning to recognize and avoid these flashpoints is another way of reducing tantrums. The more that direct conflicts can be avoided the better, because it means that future tantrum behaviour will be lessened. What must always be borne in mind is that temper tantrums, in which a toddler loses control of herself, are very frightening for the toddler herself. Despite the ill feelings that such behaviour generates, a child still needs comforting after the tantrum is over. Cuddling her at this time does not spoil her or encourage further tantrums. What you are rewarding by such cuddles is the quiet, post-tantrum, reasonable behaviour. A caregiver can use the comforting time to reinforce the alternative ways in which a toddler could have behaved and explain why throwing a tantrum is not a good idea. Refusing to comfort her as a punishment only prolongs tantrums or sparks new ones.

Growing knowledge of self

At this time, a toddler is starting to develop some idea of herself as a person – quite a complex idea that develops only gradually. One step occurs with the idea of object permanence which she has gained in the second half of her first year. With this, by implication, she develops the idea of herself as the perceiver of objects.

Another step seems to happen around fifteen months, when she seems to be able to exhibit some knowledge of what her own image is. There has been a study that investigated how a baby understood mirrors and mirror images. Babies had their noses 'wiped' by investigators. (Actually they were putting red dots on their noses.) Then the babies looked at themselves in the mirror. After fifteen months, babies focused immediately on what was wrong in the mirror image, touching their own red noses straight away as soon as they looked in the mirror.

By the second year of life, a toddler also has some understanding of her own name, and starts to use her own name or the personal pronoun 'I' or 'me'. The idea of self ties into the development of autonomy during this stage in a toddler's life. A child starts to show pleasure in mastering something for its own sake and for her own sense of worth, as well as for the reward of social approval from a caregiver. The independence drive becomes its own reward as a toddler's confidence and abilities grow and reinforce each other.

COGNITIVE DEVELOPMENT
Exploring objects

At this time, a toddler spends a lot of time in exploratory play with objects. She enjoys putting things inside containers and then taking them out again. The idea of containers is always intriguing for a toddler. As well as learning about the properties of the actual objects, a toddler is learning about spatial concepts such as inside and outside, which are tied in with the idea of object permanence. It is at this stage that a toddler achieves a true and full understanding of object permanence. She can search appropriately for an object that has disappeared out of sight, even after a time delay. This means that she must have some idea of the object in her head for guiding the search.

She is curious about the properties of things. Do they fall? bounce? tear? What happens if I shove it in here? Sometimes a child of this age seems very destructive. She likes to tear paper, take things apart, knock things down. It is important to see that it is curiosity rather than destructiveness. She enjoys pulling out the contents of purses, handbags and cupboards. Putting things back is a different and unrelated activity. Only a caregiver sees any connection between the two. It is a good idea to give a toddler a bag with an elasticated neck, which can be filled with a variety of small objects for her to pull out one by one. Alternatively, an old handbag can be filled with collections of small and interestingly shaped items. (All children seem, however, to develop a kind of sixth sense, whereby they just know that things they are given to play with, almost by definition, will not be nearly as interesting as ones they snatch for themselves without adult approval. Perhaps caregivers can try out a kind of double bluff to test this theory.)

Play with objects

The sequence of development of such play is shown in the box.

Toddlers love collecting and sorting small objects.

SEQUENCE OF DEVELOPMENT

Mouthing play: indiscriminately explores objects by mouth. Baby uses mouth movements to explore the shape, size and texture of an object.

Manipulation play: a baby uses her hands and fingers to explore objects – using visual feedback and feedback from hand movements.

Playing with the function of objects: a baby explores an object by manipulation that is appropriate for the particular object, or with the intention of extracting some bit of information, e.g. a telephone may be held up to a baby's ear.

Combining/function play: where the two objects are combined according to their appropriate use,

e.g. a lid and a stick may be brought together to make a noise.

Combining/function play: where the two objects are combined according to their appropriate use, e.g. a box and a small object may be played with by the object being put inside the box.

Pretend use: when a baby shows she knows the use of an object and can pretend with it, e.g. a baby may drink from an empty cup.

Substitution play: a baby is able to pretend that one object is something else, e.g. that a brick is a biscuit.

Changes in thinking

What kinds of toys does a child like to play with? Gradually, over her second year her preferences change. Initially, she enjoys the big, colourful, noise-making toys of a baby. Then she starts to show more of an interest in domestic objects that she sees being used around her. The way she plays changes over the course of her second year as well. She spends less time in direct exploratory play, where she uses her senses to find out about objects. This makes sense. As she learns more about more things she comes across less novelty. 'Seen that, know all about it!' The emphasis shifts from finding out about the things themselves to exploring what she can do with them. In a child's play with things we see how her mind is developing.

Problem solving

Up to about eighteen months, a baby can run through various behaviours in order to find out about the properties of things around her. First she tries one behaviour, then another. She goes through her range of behaviours in a purposeful manner. She wants to find out, but at the same time she is tied to those exploratory behaviours. Between eighteen and twenty-four months, a toddler begins to have the ability to try out behaviours in her head as it were. She does not actually have to carry them out before she can envisage whether a certain action or behaviour will solve a problem. For example, if she wants to reach a toy and there happens to be a stool nearby, she can use the stool to get the toy. She is able to think about the solution to her

This toddler demonstrates that he already knows what to do with a telephone. At this age, it is common for toddlers to know when a toy represents an everyday object and can play with it appropriately.

Toddlers can participate in early pretend play like this little girl feeding her doll. They are able to attribute life to an inanimate object, such as a doll. This marks an important development in their ability to play in a pretend fashion.

problem and then, if the solution seems to work in her head, she puts it into action. So she thinks about the stool and the toy, and only moves the stool when she realizes that such a solution will work.

Deferred imitation

This is when a baby can imitate something she sees or copy some behaviour sequence, not just when she sees it but even some time later. To do this, a baby obviously needs to have some ability for mental representation of experiences. The behaviour has to be stored away in her memory and recalled when she wants to perform the action. This growing ability to represent things mentally ties in with language. When a baby learns a word, she doesn't just say it back parrot fashion at the time, she also learns to use it in appropriate contexts in the future.

Early pretend

A toddler enjoys playing with replicas of household objects which are easier for her to manipu-

late, but at this stage she would be just as happy with the real thing, although adults wouldn't.

She is interested in what goes on around her and she loves to imitate the activities she sees being performed around her – sweeping floors, driving a car – but she is copying actions rather than pretending.

At this stage, a toddler sometimes pretends to do something, for example, to drink from an empty cup. Here she knows that she is not really getting a drink, and she is not really expecting a drink. But she is showing not only that she knows what a cup is for but that she can play around with it. Such pretence means she has some idea of a real/not real distinction. Some researchers have focused on the gestural quality of this behaviour, seeing in it a kind of naming but through action rather than word. It is more a communication of knowledge about the object than a pretend behaviour. Certainly this kind of behaviour does not necessarily have the playful intent – usually signalled by smiles, looks – that is the usual accompaniment to pretend play.

About this time, however, a baby also pretends, for example, to go to sleep. Such behaviour is signalled as playful pretence. She may also pretend to eat a brick, which shows quite advanced cognitive abilities. She knows enough about both biscuits and bricks to be able to play around with them as ideas in her head. She has extracted some of the properties of a biscuit, for example, the shape and size, and is able to act as if the brick, which shares some of those properties, can share the function of the biscuit – to be eaten. Yet at the same time she knows that the brick is a brick. She doesn't really think she can eat it. She makes chewing movements but does not put the brick in her mouth.

Early pretend is interesting for the light it throws on a baby's thinking processes. In many ways, it is in pretence that she first exhibits the kind of thinking ability that she can apply to other aspects of her life only at a much later stage. This early pretend is primarily a social behaviour. It grows out of early games and interactions, and is firmly rooted in the social context of a child's relationships with her caregivers and siblings.

Quite often, it is within social contexts that a child first shows a greater level of sophistication in the way that she can think. Social development seems to be the baseline from which other cognitive skills develop, or it is in the context of social relations that thinking develops, but only later on is this applied in the non-social sphere. In the same way communication is the basic social skill that later develops into language.

LANGUAGE DEVELOPMENT

Gestures

From the second half of her first year, a baby may use gestures that have a communicative function. The baby is intending to mean something using a particular movement. She may point to gain a caregiver's attention or because she wants something. This may have developed from a reaching gesture and become further refined into an opening and closing of a hand to signal desire. By about a year, a baby may use more elaborate gestures which represent things, such as by raising an arm to signal that she wants to be picked up. She may start using symbolic gestures to represent specific things. At first these gestures are solely to do with the baby herself. They focus on her requests and desires, but they can be used to comment on objects, for example, she may blow to indicate that something is hot. As a baby learns the word for an idea, then the importance of gestures diminishes and she tends to stop using them.

First words

A baby usually comes out with her first word at around the end of her first year or the start of her second, using a single word to express a complete thought. The meaning of the one-word utterance depends on the context in which she utters it. Initially, a caregiver has to use the context, and perhaps any accompanying gestures, to interpret the correct meaning. So, for example, 'cup!' may mean several things depending on other communicative signals. Sometimes it might mean 'Oh, look at that lovely new cup'. At others, it might mean 'Give me the contents of that mug quickly, before I die of thirst'.

What kind of words are these first words? Typically, the first words refer to things in a baby's immediate environment – mum, dad, milk – things that are important to her and that she hears most often, although sometimes it is the degree of interest that may prompt the production of a word – dog seems to be a common first word even when the animal is not a feature of a baby's usual domestic environment. Names of things are most common, although a baby will often also say 'bye-bye' and an emphatic 'no!' quite early on.

At first a baby seems to learn each new word quite slowly, often taking about four months from the utterance of the first word before a baby's vocabulary increases very much.

Then, during the second half of her second year, there is something of a naming explosion

This baby obviously wants something to be given to her. An open hand gesture is used at this age to mean 'Give it to me', and other symbolic gestures will start to be used. Once the necessary words are learned, gestures are used less.

when a toddler's learning of new words suddenly seems to take off. Her vocabulary will increase during this period from say about twenty words at eighteen months to about two hundred at twenty-one months and about four hundred by the time a toddler enters her third year.

In the second half of her second year, she may also start to combine words into two-word sentences, and this is sometimes called *telegraphic speech*. Like a telegram, such speech is compressed and does not use filler words like 'the' and 'an' or pronouns. As with the earlier one-word utterances, the meaning of a toddler's telegraphic utterances often has to be interpreted from its context. During her second year, however, a baby also tries hard to be understood.

If a caregiver is being particularly obtuse, then even an eighteen-month-old may adapt what she says in order to convey a particular meaning.

Role of adults in language learning

There are features of baby talk that caregivers typically use when talking to young babies which help focus attention on voice and those aspects of speech sounds that are most important for language understanding.

With older babies and toddlers, an adult also typically alters his speech in ways that take account of the baby's level of language comprehension. In these modifications the aim is to be understood. It was found in studies that, if an adult's language was either too unfamiliar to a child or much more complicated than the child's own, then a child just did not attend to it. If a child does not attend then she is not going to learn from it.

In speaking to toddlers, typically a caregiver usually uses shorter utterances and emphasizes key words. He uses simple constructions and lots of repetitions. By adjusting his speech to fit with the child's own level of understanding, a caregiver hopes to make his meaning as clear as he can. He is also, however, providing the best kind of set-up for learning about language itself. The properties of this kind of modified child-directed speech make it easier for a child to learn language.

Features of child-directed speech

What are the features of modified adult speech that make it helpful to a child just starting to use and understand language? They tend to use a restricted vocabulary so that a child hears the same words referring to the same object over and over again. If a dog is always a dog, rather than sometimes a hound or canine or collie, then a baby finds it easier initially to match the word with the object. Of course this will then tend to be reflected in the baby's own speech. One of the characteristic errors that we see in a young child's speech is *over-extension of terms* – one example being the baby who gets the idea that any four-legged animal is a dog.

Caregivers also tend to use the present tense when talking to babies and talk about things that are present or in the here and now. This facilitates the linking of the language used to what the language is referring to. It may seem so obvious to mature speakers of a language – so obvious that we are unaware of it – but this aspect of language has to be learned. The links between movements of mouth and tongue and flow of controlled breath and the sound patterns hitting an ear, and the wide world of objects, actions, intentions and thoughts, are various, variable and infinitely complicated.

These links have to be forged by a baby through repeated exposure. Caregivers try to help establish these links by simplifying their own speech and using as many other ways as possible to reinforce the semantic links. Context is one of the basic ways of conveying meaning. This is what we rely on if, as adults, we are ever adrift in a foreign land. We try and use the clues of context to try and understand what is being talked about, even when we cannot understand a word of what is being said.

Such adjustments to their speech are tied to their expectations about the child's developmental level. This may mean, for example, that they choose to use a word that is easy to say rather than a more difficult one. They have no problem in pronunciation but realize what limitations a baby may have. They use words knowing that babies may try and say them themselves. This sometimes explains the use by caregivers of babyisms like 'choo-choo'. Caregivers want to encourage babies to use words and therefore use a baby's own existing vocabulary to focus attention and help get meaning across, or they use words that they think babies find easy because they avoid certain sounds. Beginning talkers often find certain sounds, for example, 'th', 'sh', 'r', hard to articulate.

Caregivers may also use features from a baby's own style of talk. Such features reflect the baby's own playing around with language sounds as in, for example, the repetitions of sounds and redoubling of syllables – dada, mama.

Caregivers also adjust their speech to fit with their expectations about a child's cognitive level. This is why they talk about the here and now and the things that a baby finds interesting. The things a baby finds most interesting are also those things that she tends to look at or tries to talk about. The best adjustment a caregiver can make is actually in terms of the content. When he focuses on what it is the child is playing with or attending to and makes that the subject of his utterance, this is the most facilitative situation in which a child can learn about language.

Responding to a child's speech

It is important that a caregiver always responds to a child's attempts at communication. The first thing we want all children to have is a firm idea that talking and meaningful communication are things that we value. If we value them then they are worthy of attention. A child must learn that it is an important activity, and also that her efforts have merit. A child must develop an unshakeable confidence in her own self and in her abilities.

Models

Every time we speak to a baby, we are providing a model for her. Even when we use baby talk such speech is still correct in both grammar and meaning. The more we talk to her, the greater the opportunities she has to learn from our speech. What is even more helpful for a child learning language is when we take her utterances and, if they are incorrect in some way, give the corrected version back to her again. This doesn't mean we should predicate the corrected version by saying 'No it's not . . . but . . .', as that would defeat the point entirely, and the child would then hear you saying the incorrect version first. Also it would be unnecessarily hurtful to a child to have her errors pointed out in this way. It is helpful, however, to respond to a child's utterance by using this as the starting point for your own comment.

Expansion and recasting

When a caregiver talks directly to a child who is starting to learn language, there are ways in which the conversational situation and how the caregiver responds may help the learning process for the child. Two ways of responding have been found to be most beneficial for a child learning language: both start with the child herself – her own utterance about her own topic. This is an important feature

Recasting the utterance of a child means re-forming her sentence or phrase into a different form – perhaps adding a greater level of complexity. A caregiver could, for example, take the child's two-word sentence 'Drink juice' and respond with the question 'Do you want to have a drink of juice?'. By keeping the key words of a child's utterance, a caregiver reinforces the child's meaning and the fact that she does have *communicative competence*. By recasting a child's utterance, a caregiver is showing how to phrase it in a more grammatical form. The caregiver might go on to ask 'What kind of juice would you like to drink?'. Here, the caregiver is modelling other forms of questions again within the same semantic topic. A caregiver is modelling a more complex syntax and a child is learning about word order, grammar and meaning.

Expansion of a child's utterance is a very helpful way of giving a child experience both of wider vocabulary items and of different ways of thinking about the topic of the utterance. By starting from a child's own utterance, a caregiver has her attention already established for his own comment. Before a conversation can happen, this kind of joint attention always has to take place. Expanding on a child's utterance leads to a joint topic of conversation, in which a caregiver can use the child's own knowledge to encourage her to talk about other related subjects. If, for example, a baby says 'Dog!', then a caregiver can go on to say 'Yes, that's a big hairy dog, isn't it? Look at his tongue hanging out of his mouth. Do you see his tongue? You've got a pink tongue as well, haven't you? Can you show me your tongue?'. The caregiver uses questions to prompt the child and keep her attention. He knows the child's understanding of certain words, for example, tongue, and can bring them out to reinforce her previous learning. At the same time, he may introduce a new term such as 'pink' which the child doesn't understand at this stage. But, after meeting the same term in several different contexts and in lots of other conversations, a child comes to understand what pink means as well.

*Singing and action rhymes and one-to-one games with a caregiver can help
a child's early language development.*

Direct instruction

Children normally learn language without being
directly taught by a caregiver. They learn the
form of language and the rules through experience of listening and exposure to adult
conversation.

Some aspects of a language are, however,
taught directly by adults. These tend to be the
conventions, polite terms used in day-to-day
speech, for example, thank you, good-bye, hello,
please, thank you, pardon me. What is being
taught is really a polite behaviour form. The
words either constitute the behaviour or the tag
that goes with it.

Other words that are directly taught may be
names of things. A child goes through a time
when her vocabulary expands very rapidly
and she asks for the names of new things.

Colour terms and number terms may also
be directly taught to a child, but, on the whole,
direct instruction doesn't really play a big part in
a child's acquisition of language.

Language learning situations

A child learns language competence within a
communicative framework, and this is most
helpful when it is a situation that has a lot of
meaning for a child. Familiar daily occurrences,
which have their own regular routines and
regular objects, and actions tend to be the best
contexts for learning the associated language.

Bath time, mealtimes and bedtime all have
their routines. A baby soon learns to anticipate
what is going to happen, in what order things

will happen and what things will be used. If you use these situations to talk about what is going on and name the objects and comment on what is happening, then a baby soon learns the language associated with these routines. This can be the down-to-earth practical language as well as any rhymes or songs that may also have become part of these daily routines. Such social routines, in which a caregiver and child engage in interactions, provide a kind of structure that helps the emergence of language skills.

Games, songs and rhymes

Language is always learned in a context and some of the most enjoyable contexts for both caregivers and toddlers can be the little games that have formed part of the behaviours from the earliest days. Games with a sequence of repetitive steps, leading to a climax such as 'Round and round the garden', will have been enjoyed by a baby from her earliest months and

as she has developed so will her appreciation of the different aspects of such games. As her skills have developed, she has got more out of the game and has learned different things from it. Games themselves can evolve and change to fit in with a baby's development – they may become more complex, add more steps. The baby's role can also alter. She may become the instigator of the game or vary her role to become the active rather than the passive participant.

Nursery rhymes and songs can be appreciated from very early on, and yet they also fulfil a language learning role. Part of their helpfulness resides in their very familiarity, part in the style of language. A baby appreciates and enjoys listening to the rhyming, rhythms and repetition. A toddler can join in because of those very features of the language that make it particularly attractive to listen to. With nursery rhymes, the language features are more important than the meaning, which is why they continue to entertain children down through the generations.

Here a mother is playing 'Round and round the garden' with her son. This is a game that generations of babies have enjoyed playing.

CHAPTER FIVE

THE YOUNG CHILD

two to three years

MOTOR DEVELOPMENT
Walking tall

By two years, or after a certain amount of walking practice, a child can walk without looking at his feet and with a much more stable balance. His legs come closer together, looking more like a normal walk, and his walking appears smoother. He takes longer strides which makes his walk look more like that of an adult.

During his third year a child learns to jump in the air with both feet off the ground, although this also depends on the child's strength and co-ordination. He masters jumping down a step before jumping on the level because it takes less muscle strength, but he can run in a straight line and his running becomes true running, which involves a brief separation of the feet from the ground.

He can climb stairs but doesn't use alternate feet yet, like an adult, and needs to hold onto something or somebody. By three, he may be able to alternate his feet going upstairs, but coming back down could still be a problem. He still puts two feet together on each step coming down.

By two years, a child has developed greater hand–eye co-ordination. A child can now build blocks into structures which demonstrates his fine motor skills.

Play in water, at bath time and other times, gives good practice in fine motor skills.
Here children are learning to pour liquid from one container to another.

Fine motor skills

Turning and twisting motions (fine motor skills) using wrists, hands and fingers develop over the course of a child's third year. A two-year-old may not be able to rotate a jigsaw puzzle piece in order to get it to fit, and uses brute force instead. A three-year-old, however, has the fine motor control for manoeuvring pieces successfully. Development of this kind of skill can be helped by practising with screwing and unscrewing jars or large screws.

At this stage a child can stack blocks one on top of another, and can eat using utensils. All these show the development of his hand–eye co-ordination. He is very interested in practising newly acquired motor skills, and enjoys trying to pour liquids into cups; as this requires not only good motor control but also quite a bit of understanding of the physics of liquid flow, there are bound to be a few accidents. A child can practise pouring in his bath or in a sink of water with lots of different sized containers and different shaped spouts, and this gives a child the opportunity to learn a lot. He may also enjoy the action of pouring other substances with different flow properties, such as sand or rice. When a child is given plenty of opportunity to practise all of his fine motor skills, he develops confidence in his own abilities, and in time gains mastery of them. At this stage a child's motor development reflects not only his physical maturation, but also his experience, confidence and, in some areas, his courage.

Scribbles

At first a child may hold a crayon or pencil in a full fist grip with all his fingers wrapped around the implement. At this stage it is often easier for him to manipulate thick chunky crayons than fine pencils, as the leads of the fine pencils often break if put under any pressure.

As he gets older, a child can hold a pencil or crayon in a precision grip between fingers and thumb, which gives him much more control of the pencil. A lot of early drawings reflect a child's lack of motor control rather than any inability to understand what objects look like. Children love to scribble using a pencil or crayon and may have to be encouraged to keep their scribbles to particular places, that is, drawing paper or books rather than walls and floors. Their first scribbles tend to be from side to side, then up and down and have more to do with the enjoyment of movement than any attempt at representing objects. It is good for children to have a wide experience of using different shapes and sizes of pencils, fibretips, crayons at this stage, while they are still mastering their grip and motor control. The process of scribbling, rather than the end-product, is of interest at this stage – for the child, mastery of motor co-ordination is the main concern.

COGNITIVE DEVELOPMENT
Memory

A young baby is limited very much to the here and now; any memory processing involves recognition, for example, if something is presented to him he may be able to recognize it as somehow familiar, and in this way he can remember it. If it has not been presented to him, however, then he cannot bring it to mind or recall it.

By two years, a child is able to use recall much more. He can store memories away and then produce them at a later date; he does not need the prompt of something being presented to him. He remembers an action that he has seen an adult make and can perform that action himself at some later date. The whole behaviour is recalled.

Later on memories are often stored in a processed form. Information that is stored in the brain is organized in a meaningful way, making it easier to use the memories. Links and connections between memories reflect the way in which memories are organized and interact with the processing activity. For example, a child can use verbal labels to help him store mental representations and bring objects to mind.

During these years, children develop from holding a crayon in a full fist grip to using a precision grip. Experience of crayon, pencil or felt-tip pen for scribbles and drawing helps them in the practice of movement control.

PLAY ACTIVITIES

PLAYING SIMPLE GAMES can be a way of helping the development of memory skills in a child. For example, a caregiver can hide a small number of different items under a cloth and then ask a child to try to remember what they are. The number of items can be increased as he becomes more skilful at the game.

A child can also be encouraged to develop his strategies for remembering through participation in day-to-day activities such as shopping. He can try to remember his own list of items, perhaps using his own drawings as prompts.

LANGUAGE DEVELOPMENT

Sounds

Between the age of two and three, a child's language develops rapidly. Articulation of sounds improves so that, by about three, his speech can usually be understood by other adults. If a child is not understood immediately he attempts to modify his utterances to aid communication. He still commonly has difficulty with some sounds – consonant clusters tend to be the sounds that are the hardest for him. These are usually difficulties of production rather than of perception, however. If a caregiver repeats back the child's mispronunciation, he can hear that it is wrong:

'No, not "cwisp" – I said "cwisp"!'

If the problem is one of articulation, making a fuss about a child's mispronunciation has little effect. It doesn't help and could make a child feel inhibited at an age when he especially needs to feel happy and confident about expressing himself in order for his language to develop to its full potential. Articulation difficulties are very common and very rarely worth worrying about, as children soon grow out of them. It is a good idea to avoid making a big issue out of something like this, because it can be counterproductive. It is much more important to encourage a child to express himself than to correct the particular sounds he has difficulty with. Encourage him to practise these particular sounds. This is best done within the context of rhymes, games or songs, so that the child does not feel any pressure. Individual sounds can often be practised by, for example making animal noises – the 'sss' of a snake, the 'rrrr' of a roaring lion.

It is also useful for a child to play games that help him to control his breathing. From babyhood, he will enjoy playing blowing games. One basic game can start from getting the child simply to blow on a caregiver to tickle him, in response to similar tickle blowing from the caregiver. He can then be encouraged to blow a feather or a small piece of paper. As he gets older he might enjoy blowing a paper boat across water, blowing bubbles through a ring or frothing liquid by blowing through a straw. Blow football, or a simpler version using a ping pong ball being manoeuvred around table-top obstacles, is a game that is enjoyable for children, but at the same time it helps them to develop control over the force and direction of their breathing. Practice in making such conscious control may help later on if a child has articulation difficulties or other speech impediments to overcome.

Words

Children communicate with adults from an early stage. They don't wait until they know exactly how to say something before they attempt to do so. To communicate with a limited number of words, a child relies on using the words that he already has at his command. He tends therefore to use the words that he has for referring to other similar things, for example, he says 'dog' when pointing at a sheep.

Blowing bubbles helps a child to control his breathing which, in turn, helps with articulation. Blowing bubbles together with a caregiver can also be fun.

A child may also coin many new words, in the beginning, to fill gaps in his vocabulary and to communicate his intended meaning. Typically he uses compounds of words that he already knows to create new words, for example, 'daddy-telly' for 'computer'. These innovative terms are eventually replaced as a child hears the conventional term and incorporates it into his vocabulary. At this time a child's vocabulary is expanding rapidly. Now that he understands the idea of a word being the name of an object, he has an insatiable hunger to know the names of everything.

A child also, however, has some organizational system and uses some underlying pragmatic principles to govern the addition of words to his vocabulary. For example, a child usually takes up the normal adult term for something, rather than an idiosyncratic and one-off usage. He uses the adult word forms that he hears and uses them consistently. He follows the conventions of the language where a word has an agreed meaning shared by users of that language and does not change that meaning arbitrarily. When a child first starts to talk he may use the word 'dog' to refer to lots of different animals; as he starts to learn the correct names of things, he uses only the words that he hears an adult use for a particular animal. At this stage in his language development, a child also stops naming things if he doesn't know the conventional words.

When a child corrects his own speech, often (about 40% of the time for two- to three-year-olds) the corrections involve changes in word choices (Clark, 1982). Children try to use the correct word, that is, the word that they hear an adult use normally.

There is another pragmatic principle that a child also uses to govern how he adds words to his vocabulary, involving some idea of difference or contrast. When a child adds a new word he assumes that it is at the same descriptive level but has a different meaning. So the new word is treated as if it contrasts with a word that is already known. In this way a new word cuts down on the over-extension of word meaning that a child employs to begin with. Instead of just 'dog', he uses 'cow' or 'sheep' or 'pig' or 'elephant' as his vocabulary increases, all these words referring to different kinds of four-legged animals. At the start, a child sees each new word as having a distinct new meaning and a contrasting meaning to those words that he already knows, that is, if a term differs in form then it must differ in meaning. This gives a one-to-one mapping of meaning to form. A child does not accept several different words for the same object, but assumes that all labels are on the same level of naming and do not overlap. This explains why he has difficulty with labels that refer to different levels, for example, 'animal' and 'dog' or 'brick' and 'toy'. He does not understand the contrast in their meaning. A known conventional word is given priority, so 'dog' takes priority over 'animal' to begin with. A child is very unlikely to use a word like 'animal' to refer to something that he already has a label for, for example, 'dog'. A word like 'cow' is alright, however, because it has a contrasting meaning to 'dog' and it is acquired rapidly by the child. He soon learns to give distinct verbal labels to distinct animals.

It is a good idea to encourage a child to learn the name of any new object he comes across, and also to make a game out of his growing list of names for things so that he can be encouraged to recite, for example: all the names of different animals that he knows; the names of all the animals that he knows live on a farm; all those that live in a zoo. This encourages him to start thinking about sorting into different categories and different levels of names.

Only as a child develops does he come to understand that words exist at different levels. A word and its meaning may not have the simple mapping of an object to its name, but has relationships with other words and labels. The concept of a 'dog' as an 'animal' is very hard for a child to take on board, because it violates one of the rules that he uses for organizing new words into his expanding vocabulary.

Grammar

During his third year, a child starts to use simple three-or four-word sentences, and his knowledge and understanding increase of the rules by which words are organized. Through listening to adult language, a child gradually notices patterns in the way language is put together, for example, he notices that adding '-s' to a word means that it refers to more than one. In this way a child learns the grammar of his native language. At the start, he makes errors of over-extending or over-generalizing rules. A child will say 'mouses' rather than 'mice' even though he has never heard the word 'mouses' used by adults.

In a way, it is these very errors that show us how clever a three-year-old is. They show us how he can analyse the language he hears, notice similarities and constancies, and then derive the underlying rules governing that language. He then applies these rules in a systematic way to produce new combinations. In terms of meaning, these previously unheard utterances make sense. Rules for producing past tenses of verbs are also over-extended, and he may say 'I falled down' rather than 'I fell'. The child learns, by experience, all the exceptions to the regular rules of syntax. Much of this learning occurs during dialogue with a caregiver, when the caregiver restructures a child's sentences in a more correct grammatical form.

During his third year a child starts to move the words around in a sentence in order to make negative statements or questions. Initially, a child uses 'wh-' words to ask questions without rearranging the words: 'When we go out?' rather than 'When are we going out?'. The question is marked solely by the 'wh-' word at the start, sometimes with a rising intonation of the voice. Later he uses the correct word order for questions.

During this period, a child is learning an awful lot about language; he is very interested in understanding others and expressing himself. He also starts to use language as a means of self-regulation, by telling himself off or using words to comfort himself. Language is starting to be the medium of his own thinking.

Playing with language

A child is also interested in language for its own sake. He likes rhymes very much and soon enjoys playing about with words and rhymes on his own. A child often talks to himself – before falling asleep at night, for example. At this age, he may play around with different sounds to create nonsense words. This kind of language play, usually during a child's reflective relaxation (down time), probably helps him to integrate and organize the vast amount of new language information that he is absorbing.

It is important to encourage this kind of language play. A child is setting the foundations for later literacy skills through such play. Noticing rhyme and similar sounds helps a child when he comes to learn to read, because, in reading, he has to discriminate not only the visual patterns of letters and words, but also the sound patterns that those letters represent. It is helpful for a child to have an ability to hear similarities and differences in words and parts of words. This kind of sound discrimination can be learned through enjoyment of rhymes and is the best way for children to practise. Research has revealed that children who have early experience with nursery rhymes are more successful later in reading than those who do not have such experience.

Reading, reciting and singing rhymes to a child help his language development and his future abilities for learning to read. Children

PLAY ACTIVITY

Singing games that use question forms and then answer the questions can help a child's language development, for example:

Tommy thumb, Tommy thumb
Where are you?
Here I am, here I am
How do you do?

Also the script of ritual games can often be used to model correct question forms:

Where's the Teddy? Here he is!
Who is this hidden under the cushion? It's Teddy!
When is that Jack-in-the-Box going to pop?
Now!

love learning rhymes both new and old. Often the favourite bedtime listening is tapes of rhymes and songs. Children's songs with a strong rhythmic beat and sound rhymes encourage his language skills at many different levels. The personal rhymes that a caregiver or a child may make up on the spur of the moment come into a special category, however. In particular he enjoys making up simple rhymes to share with a caregiver. Playing around with words is not just silliness; it shows an awareness of language that reflects a child's growing cognitive development. The ability to produce rhyming words is associated with early reading achievement.

Enjoying stories

Babies can enjoy sharing a picture book with a caregiver from a very early age. It combines a form of relaxed down time with physical closeness, and this is most enjoyable for busy adults and busy children alike. It also forms a joint attention activity which creates the best kind of environment for learning about language. Younger children enjoy brightly coloured, clear, realistic illustrations; they can then use these to learn names, enjoying pointing to the relevant things, and naming and discussing them. They enjoy the sequence of look, talk, turn the page. As a picture book becomes more familiar they enjoy predicting what will come when a page is turned as they are familiar with the sequence and enjoy joining in. A picture book can be the focus of turn-taking conversations with even quite young children.

As children get older they enjoy the sequence of an unfolding story line. First one thing happens, then another, and so on. This is something that develops from quite a young age and even babies enjoy a simple story. As a picture book becomes more familiar, enjoyment comes with recognition of the pattern of events and predicting what is going to happen next. As children get even older, they enjoy more complicated stories; they soon develop favourites which they enjoy hearing read again and again. They are often able to catch you out if you try and skip any bits in order to hurry things along.

Listening to a story is not just a pleasant way of passing the time for a child. In fact he is learning the skills that make learning to read easier. When a child learns to read, he learns to read a story, so familiarity with the story form gives him an advantage. Beginning readers use the context in which the written word appears

Sharing books with your child from an early age provides him with a head start in development of basic literacy skills because he already understands that reading is an enjoyable and important activity.

to obtain clues about the meaning of the words. If a child has lots of stories read to him, he will already be an expert at reading the clues, that is, the pictures, in order to understand the meaning in the book.

A three-year-old often surprises a caregiver by sitting down and 'reading' a familiar book to himself. He has already learned the use of context for meaning, and has a good memory of what the story is about. He may even remember the story sequence and the words and phrases used in the book. He starts from the beginning, moving his eyes from left to right across the page because this is what he has seen a caregiver do. He may even move his fingers under the words, although there is often no correspond-ence between the finger points and the words he utters. He is not really reading the book, but nor is he just mimicking his caregiver's behavi-our. He is demonstrating that he has already acquired many of the essential pre-reading skills which will help him when he comes to learn to read.

It is often in the context of a favourite story that a child first recognizes a word that occurs again and again. He can read that word every time you come to it in that story. Sometimes he may even learn to recognize it if it occurs in different stories.

Sometimes it is the shape of the individual letters that a child first recognizes. He may associate the shape with the sound he hears and then come to name the letter with the sound. With alphabet books, it is a good idea to try and reinforce the link between letter and sound by using the letter sound rather than the letter name as you point to each individual letter.

The main thing achieved by reading a lot to a child is, however, getting over the idea that reading stories is a valued and important activity. When you read a story to a child you are also acting as a model for that child. He sees you as an example not only of a competent reader, but also of someone who thinks that reading is important and enjoyable. This idea of reading as a valued activity and books as a

natural thing to have around the home – a caregiver's attitude towards reading – is the most predictive factor for a child's own later reading success.

UNDERSTANDING CONCEPTS

A child develops an understanding of certain abstract ideas or concepts only through familiarity and experience. The concept of an object is one that develops over time and through a baby's exploration of a wide variety of objects. There are many concepts that adults take for granted which develop gradually through experience.

The concepts of quantity, size, shape, colour, identity and number are complex. Often the language connected with such concepts is deceptively simple. 'Big', 'bigger', 'more', 'less', 'same', 'different' are words that are used by adults to children, often without considering the difficulty that a child may have in fully under-standing what the terms mean.

A child may use such terms without a caregiver realizing that he doesn't fully under-stand their meaning. It is important to be aware of how hard some ideas can be for a child and the ways that can be used to help him to develop his understanding. Throughout a child's pre-school years and beyond, his understanding of abstract ideas will develop.

Colour

It is only through experience of hearing the colour term 'red' used with a wide variety of red coloured objects, which may of course vary in softness, hardness, size, shape, smell, touch and familiarity, that a child gradually starts to develop understanding of the concept of redness. If you consider all the ways that objects may vary, then you can understand that it is not easy for a child to focus on what we mean when we use a colour label. It is only with the widest

A child's own clothing makes a good starting point for the introduction of colour terms into her vocabulary, as well as providing practice in the development of the motor skills involved in dressing.

experience of hearing the terms used appropriately that a child can gradually focus on the particular aspect that we mean when we refer to the colour of something. It is very important for a caregiver to help the process by using colour terms whenever possible and whenever appropriate. Using colour labels when talking about things helps a child learn to focus on that aspect of an object's properties and reinforces any learning of the colour term.

A child's own clothing is often a good starting point for introducing colour terms into a conversation. Over time children understand

colour and increase their vocabulary of colour terms. A child can differentiate colours and match similarly coloured objects before he knows the correct colour term for an object. Colour matching games in which objects have to be sorted into, for example, two groups on the basis of colour – preferably primary colours – make a good start in helping a child to understand the concept of colour. First, the child is helped to sort the items on the basis of colour; then the colour term is introduced as part of the sorting process. Only later, when the child feels competent at distinguishing on the basis of

This child is being shown how to count using a brightly coloured abacus.
Children should be encouraged to count everything: steps as they walk along;
spoonfuls as they eat; and beads and other small items that they play with.

colour, is he asked to label items with the appropriate colour terms. Again it is important that such requests form part of a game.

Idea of shape

As with colour, a child gradually understands the idea of shape. He needs to have a wide experience of different shapes to explore with his mouth, hands and eyes; he also needs to hear shape terms used consistently and appropriately by caregivers, so that eventually he associates particular words, such as round, straight, square and triangle, with what he experiences. Children learn best through the use of three-dimensional objects that they can explore by touch and sight. They need activities in which they manipulate geometric shapes. Through play with building bricks and blocks, balls and other toys, children explore the properties of these objects and gain

some understanding of shape. Only later do they associate pictures of real shapes with the three-dimensional objects themselves and identify abstract symbols.

There are many toys that give children experience with different simple geometric shapes, such as posting boxes, although often a child learns to perform a certain set of actions from these toys rather than to derive more abstract concepts. They also need adult input to expand the activity into a wider learning experience. A caregiver can use the opportunity to talk about shape, to use the different shape names and to focus on attributes that distinguish the different shapes. This also provides a good opportunity for widening a child's perception. He can be encouraged to look around and focus on other features of his environment which may share similar characteristics or shapes; a caregiver can talk about other things that have the same shape, or a child can be encouraged to find something that looks the same. Toys then act as the springboard to a wider learning experience.

Size

The concepts of big and small, tall and short are other ideas that a child gradually understands more fully during his pre-school years. Again he needs to have an opportunity to hear the terms used in appropriate and consistent situations in which the meaning is as clear and simple as possible. The concept of comparative terms such as big, bigger, biggest is not easy. After all, a word like 'big' can refer to such a wide variety of things: a three-year-old can be a 'big boy' when compared with a new baby, but a 'little boy' when he is not allowed to do something that his elder brother does.

As with colour, a picture book can often help to give a child the experience of such terms and concepts in an enjoyable way. Traditional tales such as 'Goldilocks and the Three Bears' reinforce the idea of different size terms by repetition, and there are many modern picture books that also use the idea of different size terms as the basis of their stories.

Concept of number

The concept of number is a hard one for a child to grasp and one that he develops only through a wide experience of hearing the number name in association with various different groups of objects which all correspond to that particular number name.

Initially, a child needs to learn the number names as names. Then he learns the number names in their right order and only much later does he learn that there is a one-to-one correspondence between a number name and a group of objects making up that particular number. This last is what we mean by a concept of number – the idea of what a number means. Before a child can develop any concept of number he has to learn the number

names and this can be done through endless practice in counting things and also in learning number rhymes, for example:

One, two buckle my shoe
Three, four knock at the door
Five, six pick up sticks
Seven, eight lay them straight

One two three four five,
Once I caught a fish alive.
Six seven eight nine ten,
Then I let it go again.
Why did you let it go?
Because it bit my finger so.

A child should be encouraged to count everything – steps going up and down stairs, paces as he walks along the street, the number of buses passing the window, the number of toys in a box. It is only through repetitive counting that he learns the number names and realizes what they mean. To start with, even after a child has learned number names, he does not match them with, for example, the number of steps he takes. He may well have reached number five in his count while only having taken three steps.

At the same time as games to practise counting, it is also useful for a child to play matching, grouping and sorting games with collections of different objects. A child has to learn the concepts of 'more' and 'less' and 'same' and 'different' if he is to gain a full understanding of number. He also needs to learn the relationship of numbers to each other – that six is less than seven and more than five – and to understand that such relationships don't just refer to name order, but match the different sizes of groupings and sets of objects.

Just as learning to recite the alphabet does not mean that a child can read, so learning to recite a list of numbers does not mean that a child understands number.

At this early stage a child may only understand what one or two means, although able to recite his numbers up to ten or more.

SOCIAL DEVELOPMENT

Pretend play

In a play group, a young child may sit at a table engrossed in building a tower with blocks. It is easy for adults to see the educational value of such play: we see the concentrated expression on his face, we watch as his fingers exercise recently acquired manipulative skills, his eyes scan the blocks on the table, and he uses judgement to select a particular one, may perhaps discard another and try yet a third. We can relate to all this as adults and often use similar skills in our everyday life. We recognize the activity as play, but at the same time we can see that it is purposeful and in lots of ways a constructive and educational activity.

Meanwhile some other children are playing in the home corner. They are similarly engrossed in their activity, with expressions of concentration on their faces and seem to be unaware of events going on around them. One boy turns from a pretend cooker with a building block in his hand. He hands it to another who is sitting at a table. That child says 'Thank you!' and raises the block to his lips. Keeping it just touching his lips he says 'Yum, yum. Nice biscuit!' and pretends to eat the building block.

In such a situation it is much harder for us to see what the child is learning through such play, or to understand what skills he might be practising. Quite often it seems as if the child is just mimicking the behaviour of those he sees around him, whereas in fact there are creative aspects to such play and it draws upon a high level of thinking skills.

A skilled social performer

In the pretend play scenario a child is demonstrating advanced social skills. He is interacting successfully with another human being, co-operating in a joint endeavour and adjusting his behaviour to fit the other child's imaginary schemes. Quite often we undervalue such social skills by concentrating more on language and cognitive abilities as indicators of intelligence and developmental progress (unless there is some deficiency or failure in the child's acquiring of a range of social behaviours, social skills are ones that we don't really notice unless they're not there).

An advanced thinker

Apart from the use of social skills in pretend play, there is also some pretty sophisticated thinking going on. Indeed, in pretence, children's thinking shows a higher level of complexity than in any other aspect of their lives.

What is a child doing when he pretends that a block is a biscuit? Well, to start with, he is very much aware that he is pretending. This level of awareness is unusual and at this stage is not a typical feature of a child's development.

By pretending a child is aware of his own mental state. When he pretends with others, he is also aware that they are pretending – and that they have a particular mental outlook. This assignment of mental states to others is something that a child is not yet able to do in other aspects of life.

For example, when asked what mum would like as a present, a child typically answers 'A toy tractor!' – he cannot separate his own desires from those of others. He cannot put himself into another person's shoes. In many ways he acts as if he has no theory of mind – he is unaware that other people have internal states at all.

In pretend play, a child tries out several points of view, however, and assigns mental states to others and even to inanimate objects. For a child to say 'My dolly's hungry!' requires some advanced level thinking skills.

Reality and appearance

When a child pretends that the block is a biscuit, he understands very well that a block is a block and a biscuit is a biscuit. He has a good grasp of the difference between reality and

Pretend play provides a situation in which children can develop their social skills. In pretend play, children demonstrate some quite sophisticated thinking skills.

appearance. The block may look like a biscuit, he may lift it to his lips and make eating gestures, but he will not really try and eat the block. The level of thinking skill shown in pretend play is one that the child has not yet reached in other aspects of life.

Children cannot separate appearance from

reality, as exhibited, for example, in objects that look like something else (that is, illusory). In one study, three- and four-year-olds were shown sponges that had been painted to look like rocks. The four-year-olds had no trouble separating appearance from reality, but the three-year-olds found the task very difficult. Either they claimed that the object both looked like a rock and was a rock or they claimed that as it was a sponge then it looked like a sponge. They could not ascribe two identities to a single object at the same time.

This type of thinking also shows up in language skills. It explains some of the difficulties that younger children have in learning particular kinds of words, particularly those associated with classes and categories. Once a child has learned that something is called a 'cat', he is biased against accepting that it can also be labelled 'animal' or 'pet'. This difficulty relates to an inability to understand that something can be interpreted in many ways.

In pretend play, however, even quite young children have no trouble with the idea that a block can be both a block and a biscuit at the same time. So, in this context they can easily deal with an object having two identities.

In pretend play children do therefore show a kind of thinking skill that is in advance of its appearance in other areas; they also show an early competence for understanding mental representation. Studies have indeed shown that pretend play has an important role in the development of thinking skills in the young child.

As with other behaviour, pretend play develops as the child does. Psychologists have described different stages in the development of early pretend behaviour and these are shown in the box on page 91.

Props for pretend play

In pretend play, there is a developmental progression in the kinds of toys or props that children use. For younger children playing pretend games, the more realistic the props the easier it is for them to pretend. Very young children are happy to imitate adult behaviour using real domestic utensils. Two-year-olds enjoy using quite realistic toys where it is quite obvious what the toy is supposed to represent. They will pretend to perform some domestic task using a toy that shares many of the features

of the real object that it represents. The toys fulfil a role in sustaining a child's pretend play at this early stage. Toy cups and saucers, pots and pans, and replicas of domestic equipment encourage pretend play among younger children and help to focus it.

As a child gets older he can use non-realistic toys for playing. Later, as a child gets better at sustaining mental representations and has more verbal labels to help these representations, he can pretend without the need for realistic props. The focus moves to the child; an object becomes what is dictated by the game rather than the other way around – props determine what kind of pretend game is played. He can use objects in new and innovative ways in his pretend play: he can drink tea from a box, a scoop, a shell or even a completely invisible cup.

For these younger children, realistic toy props such as pots and pans or cups and saucers help in sustaining pretend play. As children get older they have less need of such realistic toys.

Pretending is a forum in which a child can learn about the real world of objects and social relationships, and integrate this learning into his own personal body of understanding. In such play he can expand, consolidate and transform his understanding.

Through the use of his imagination a child can create and try out new forms of social interactions and behaviours, so it is not really surprising that studies have found a relationship between a child's pretend play activity and measures of creativity.

STAGES IN DEVELOPMENT OF PRETEND PLAY

Enactive naming: this is when a child knows that a cup is for drinking and brings it to his lips even when it is empty. This is not true pretending, however, because the child is not aware of any pretence. The child is not playing; the 'pretence' is part of his language and gesture repertoire.

Autosymbolic schemes: the child pretends, but only with regard to self. He may put his head on a pillow and pretend to sleep or pretend to drink from an empty cup, smacking his lips as if really drinking. This usually starts by about twelve months.

Decentred symbolic schemes: a child may give an empty cup to a caregiver who is expected to pretend to drink. This involves an awareness of others, and usually happens between twelve and twenty-four months. At around two years, children are also able to pretend that dolls are alive. They assign fear or hunger or other mental states to an inanimate object. This seems to be an important milestone in children's thinking skills.

Sequencing pretend acts: a child is able to put pretend acts into an orderly sequence. For example, he will show that he has to take a doll's hat off before he can pretend to comb its hair.

Planned pretend: a child goes around, collecting items that he needs for a pretend play interlude.

(From McCune-Nicolich, 1981.)

CHAPTER SIX

THE PRE-SCHOOLER

three to five years

MOTOR DEVELOPMENT

From the age of three to five years, a child continues to develop control over her body. She can walk with large strides and run fast. She can jump, stand on one leg, hop and skip; she learns how to throw and catch a ball, and she may also learn how to swim, pedal a trike or a bicycle. Gross motor skill development, along with strength, balance and stamina, can vary greatly. Increasingly, a child's skill has less to do with simple maturation and more to do with opportunity, experience, practice, interest and encouragement. Not all children acquire the same skills, and levels of ability vary greatly. Some four-year-olds may already have some area of particular ability, such as ballet dancing or ice skating; others still have the residual clumsiness of a young pre-schooler. (Some recent research has indicated that dietary supplements, including fish oils, can have an improving effect on young children who have poor co-ordination.)

Fine motor control

At this stage, a child enjoys the kind of play that involves practice and mastery of her fine movement (motor) skills. This play is of great importance in her later ability to write and perform well at school. Threading beads, sewing cards, manipulating the pieces of a puzzle or pushing pegs in a pegboard all help with hand–eye co-ordination, as well as helping her to learn about sequencing of tasks, concen-

tration and perseverance. She enjoys the feeling of accomplishment that she gets when she has successfully completed a task. If a caregiver also encourages her to persevere in a task, giving praise when she has completed it, this reinforces the kinds of attitude and behaviour that lead to success in more formal learning situations.

A child enjoys such fine motor activities as hammering, screwing, scribbling, cutting, pasting, brushing, etc. She starts to gain mastery in manipulation and control of tools: pencils, brushes, eating utensils, scissors, etc. – things that require specialist grips and a high level of co-ordinated action sequences. As she gains motor control and her hand–eye co-ordination develops, she can copy shapes, letters and numbers, and build complex structures with building blocks. In terms of her own growing independence she can dress herself – being able to fasten and unfasten zips, fasteners and buttons, and later on to tie shoe laces.

Handedness

During the pre-school years, children show that the different halves of the brain are starting to perform separate functions. In general, the left hemisphere of the brain deals with processing in a linear fashion (one thing is done after another), whereas the right hemisphere deals with processing of pattern and relationships.

An individual's preference for using a particular hand for particular tasks emerges during the pre-school years, but does not

Pre-school children have more control over their bodies and greatly increased stamina and physical co-ordination. They enjoy jumping, hopping, skipping and running, all of which show the development of their gross motor skills

stabilize until about school age. There are genetic influences on handedness. If a parent is left-handed, then a child is more likely to show a preference for the left. However, the characteristics of the particular behaviours or actions often affect which hand a child uses, so that a right-handed bias is strongest for behaviours that are taught, such as eating with a spoon or using scissors. There is less right-hand bias shown in behaviours that a child learns to do on her own with no explicit teaching, such as building with bricks or digging in a sand tray.

It is important not to influence a child to use a particular hand against her natural inclination. For one thing, it can make a task doubly hard for a child, undermining her own confidence and sense of competence. This is often particularly hard when helping a child with a task for which you yourself show a strong hand dominance, for example, using scissors, where the action requires co-ordination of position and movements which a caregiver finds hard to disentangle in the attempt to explain to a child. It is best perhaps to let the child pick the scissors up herself; you can then use that hand as the starting point for any help you give her.

DEVELOPMENT OF SOCIAL PLAY BEHAVIOUR

1 Unoccupied behaviour: a child wanders around; she may watch but does not become involved in any activity for more than a moment or two.

2 Onlooker behaviour: a child watches other children playing but does not enter into the activities herself. Unlike in (1), however, she is involved in the activities as an onlooker.

3 Solitary play: a child plays alone with toys. She is neither involved with other children nor aware of them.

4 Parallel play: two or more children may play with the same toys in much the same way, next to each other. They are aware of each other's presence but they do not interact. They don't talk to each other or share the toys. They look at each other from time to time but they do not join in with each other.

5 Associative play: a child plays with other children but acts on her own rather than doing what the group wants. The children may take part in a common activity and talk to each other about it, but their activity is not co-ordinated. They are not very clear about what they are up to, and they don't tend to have particular roles or tasks within the group, so that play is not organized as a whole group.

6 Co-operative play: children form into groups in order to play a particular game – usually make believe or to accomplish some task. Children assign themselves roles within these groups and stick to these roles unless changed by negotiation within the group.

(From Parten, 1932.)

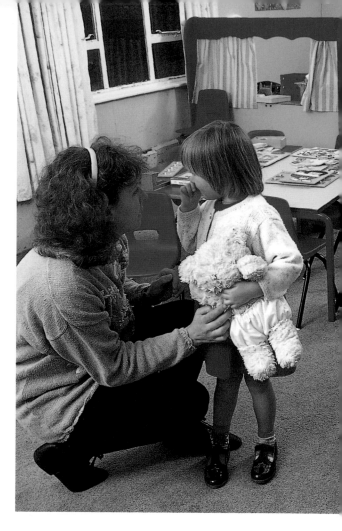

SOCIAL DEVELOPMENT
Learning to play with other children

At this stage, a child's horizons usually expand beyond the home to play groups, nurseries and schools which provide her with her first regular interaction with a much wider circle of people. This could include unfamiliar people and perhaps other children of different ages.

A child's social skills are very important because they influence how she interacts with others in a group, and the quality of these interactions. These interactions, in turn, influence the quality of a child's experiences and thus the amount and quality of all aspects of her learning – not just in development of further social skills, but also in her thinking, language and communication skills, and her intellectual development.

Social play

During the pre-school years, a child's pattern of playing changes. There is a definite progression seen in play with other children; this has been described as having six levels, as shown in the box.

The ability of a child to play socially with others is related to age, and is dependent on a child's cognitive development, language skills and emotional maturity, as well as the social skills that develop through experience of interacting with others.

There is a clear developmental progression through the six levels of social play. Infants often first imitate each other at around the end of the first year of life. In their second year, children engage in play activities with their peers when the opportunity arises. They often start to interact through parallel play (playing alongside each other). Initially, a child interacts with just one other child. In fact, two-year-olds are usually not capable of playing with more than one other child at the same time. By three, however, a child can play in a group, although most group play initially means only two or three children. As a pre-schooler gets older, the

Once a child starts nursery, her social skills become very important. These skills mediate the kind of interactions she has and therefore how much she benefits from the learning opportunities in such interactions.

Children of this age often may play alongside each other with the same toys but do not really interact. This is called parallel play.

groups get larger to become level 6 or co-operative play. This is usually seen in children in their fourth year. The amount of such social group co-operative play increases during later pre-school and early school ages before tailing off during middle childhood.

All children of varying ages can show all of the types of play categorised in the box at different times and in different situations. The same child can stand and watch, be absorbed in her own solitary activity, mimic the actions of another or join in an elaborate group pretend game – all in the course of a busy morning at nursery. She may stand back and seem completely unoccupied at times. During that time she could be thinking about what she has been doing and consolidating any new learning.

Adults also show different levels of play in their 'play' activities. Is an exercise class parallel play? Are football fans exhibiting onlooker play?

There could be large individual differences among children in their preferred style of play. Whether through temperament or circumstances, some children do not play as much with other children; this does not necessarily mean that their development in either social skills or cognitive skills is held back.

Siblings

The development of a child's ability to engage in social play with others is obviously influenced by other factors, the main one being experience. If a child has had limited opportunities to play with other children, then she is slower in developing the social interaction skills needed. Having an older sibling can make a huge difference. Even children of two or under can play collaboratively in a surprisingly sophisticated way if they have had experience of playing with older siblings from an early age.

Role of caregivers

Some settings are better for fostering collaborative play among children than others. Caregivers can often encourage such behaviour by intervening in sensitive and non-obtrusive ways. For example, at a basic level a caregiver can draw a child's attention to an activity if she seems unoccupied, encouraging her to try it. Through attention and encouragement the child may want to try something that she would not otherwise have done. A caregiver can talk to a child who is just standing by watching, and by suggestion and talking about what she is watching encourage her to join in.

If children are engaged in parallel play, it could be helpful for a caregiver to talk about what each child is doing, so showing them how they could join together. In group pretend play, younger children sometimes need help to maintain their role. A caregiver can give verbal labels which help to sustain a role, make suggestions about the different kinds of activity, and engage the children in conversations about their roles; all these reinforce and elaborate the play. Engaging in social play involves the co-ordination of lots of different social skills, including listening, talking, communicating meaning and negotiation, all of which needs to be done before the game gets started; a caregiver can therefore often help if any breakdown in communications occurs among the children.

Pretend play

Development of real life social skills
When a group of children is acting out a pretend play together, some very high level social skills are being used. In many respects, the ability to engage in group pretend play helps children to practise these social skills necessary to be successful in life.

For group pretend play, a child has to communicate effectively, that is, carry on a conversation, maintain eye contact, listen to and observe others closely, and adapt her own language to communicate her meaning. She needs to take on a role, act according to that role, and understand and respect others who are doing the same. She must take turns and act

These children need, in this group pretend play, to be able to communicate effectively with each other and co-ordinate their own behaviour to fit in with the rest – to avoid being rejected.

co-operatively towards an agreed goal. She must take part in negotiating roles with other members of the group and stick to agreed group decisions about the way in which the play develops.

We can see that these skills are indeed the kind of advanced social skills that a person needs to take a full and active part in society as an adult. A child must adjust her behaviour to fit in with a group and her own chosen role within that group. She has to be tolerant of others and their needs and desires, and able both to give and to receive help. She must have the ability to see things from others' points of view and to respond appropriately to other people. At various times she must be able to assert her own views, negotiate with others and persuade others to her opinions.

Social play can foster many socially desirable behaviours such as co-operation, sharing and abiding by agreed rules and conventions.

Pretend and emotional learning

It is surely the case that many children first try out their 'people skills' – both diplomatic and manipulative – in the home corner during pretend play. They can start by imitating what they have seen and replicate it in play. With wider experience, they learn, particularly from older children, how to expand the play in new directions. As they gain wider experience of real life situations and narrative forms, they can explore story lines in dramatic pretend play scenarios, where strong emotions such as fear and sorrow can be dealt with.

At the same time, within the 'safety net' of pretend (that is, an acknowledged 'not-for-real' situation), children can also deal with any of their own emotional difficulties and problems concerning either their own family situation or their own fears. Issues that a child may be having problems with – such as naughtiness, punishment and control – can be played around with in the non-threatening situation of pretend play. This can then help a child to sort out her own feelings about these issues.

Within pretend play a child also has the opportunity to try out lots of different roles, for example, what it must feel like to be another person. Through this playing around with the sense of what it is like to be another, a child can refine her own growing sense of self-identity.

Friendships

From an early age, children show that they like some people more than others, apart from the early development of attachment between a child and a caregiver. They can develop friend-ships with children of their own age, although often these early friendships are unstable and changeable. By three, a child moderates her own behaviour, for example, her possessiveness, in order to maintain the goodwill of other child-ren. By about four, a child's friendships become more durable. Such friendships often, however,

reflect a child's shared activities. Pre-schoolers see friendship as based on a relationship with someone who likes doing the same things as them – a friend is someone who you like to play with. Later on, at about school age, this idea shifts towards a friend as someone with a likeable disposition – someone is a friend because of what she is rather than just because of playing together.

Familiarity with playmates and friendships influence a child's behaviour. A new situation is always less anxiety provoking if a familiar playmate is present. A child prefers to explore a new environment with a familiar playmate rather than with an unfamiliar child of the same age. She is usually more skilful at taking turns with a friend than with a non-friend, and plays in a more co-ordinated way with a friend. So friendship or familiarity can mediate playing in a more developed·way. Older brothers and sisters, by being familiar and role models, similarly can influence young children's playing at a more sophisticated level.

Here are two boys who are obviously friends. Children's friendships that develop now tend to be more lasting than those developed at earlier ages.

Pre-schoolers make friends with those they like to play with rather than just someone who plays the same games.

Joining in

In a nursery or play group situation, a child may sometimes find it difficult to gain access to established on-going group play. If a child is withdrawn, she may shrink from taking the initiative needed to join in. This is where a care-giver could encourage the others to offer an invitation to join in or help the child herself to be more assertive. Different kinds of 'access rituals' exist which children seem to have to learn before they can successfully join in with group play. This is a bit like with conversations, when there is a kind of subtle timing of behaviour shifts and changes which are part of the communication necessary for joining in play with others. First a child takes some time to attend to what is going on, and then she has to signal her intention and desire to join in. After this, there is a period of unobtrusive joining in with the action – almost a kind of apprentice-ship – before a child can take a fuller role by join-ing in any negotiations and making suggestions

for how the play might develop. These social rituals can be quite subtle and there are many points at which the process can break down and a child be excluded. Caregivers can often help children avoid communication breakdowns or help a particular child to alter her behaviour in ways that give her access to group play. They can foster some useful tactics: playing unobtrusively alongside – akin to parallel playing – is one successful tactic. Another is a direct request to join in. What is not successful is if a child breaks into group play by grabbing objects or disrupting the action of the play. She is likely to be rebuffed by the group. Such a tactic usually shows lack of social skills more than anything else, as a child may not intend to be aggressive or disruptive. But, again, the cycle of such behaviour can be reinforced, because a rebuffed child is then usually excluded from situations in which she would be able to develop her social skills. She feels negative towards the group and may become even more disruptive, with this time perhaps an increase in intentional aggression.

Aggression

All pre-schoolers can show aggression at times, and it can be non-intentional as, for example, when a child takes another's toy, not because she wants to upset the other child but simply because she wants it. Other aggressive behaviours occur because a child uses physical means to get what she wants or to resolve conflicts. As a child becomes older and less reliant on the physical, aggressive behaviours should decline. She can now use verbal methods such as asking or persuading or negotiating, which avoid physical conflicts. Some children, however, even when they can use other methods, rely on physical aggression as a way of getting their own way, often because it was such a successful tactic in the past.

At the individual level, there are many influences on the frequency of aggressive behaviour. Boys tend to be more aggressive than girls. The influence of other children can play a part, as well as the media and the way a child's family behaves. Some children are temperamentally more aggressive than others. For children with difficulty controlling aggressive behaviour, a structured routine seems to be especially important. The predictability and consistency of such a routine limit the number of aggressive outbursts, as outbursts often occur in situations in which a child feels unsure of herself or does not know how she should behave. A routine provides an external structure and reduces the amount of ambiguity which might trigger the feelings that lead to aggression.

It has been shown that very aggressive children often do not deal with ambiguity very well. They may distort the cues, misinterpret quite neutral situations and react to them as if they are under threat in some way. Another child walking close by could be seen as posing some harm and she may react in an aggressive way to this perceived threat. Such children need help in understanding that they are misinterpreting situations.

There is often a pattern to the outbursts of aggressive children, and it is usually possible to discover what kinds of situations trigger the aggression. Knowing these triggers can help in dealing with the behaviour and reading the early signs of an impending outburst also helps. In both cases it is best to try to avoid the aggressive behaviour through intervention at an early stage or avoidance of triggering situations. Aggressive play is not cathartic – playing in an aggressive way does not lead to less aggressive behaviour in real life. Aggression leads to more aggression. It is therefore a good tactic to try as much as possible to avoid allowing a child to act aggressively. Early intervention is better than hoping a behaviour does not escalate into violence and aggression if allowed to continue. In general, physical punishment of a child for misbehaving is not a good idea, but if this behaviour involves aggression then it is an even worse idea. By acting in this fashion, a caregiver is at best giving out mixed and confusing signals. Punishment that is not understood by a child is not effective. Even worse, the caregiver is modelling the very behaviour he wants to discourage, so that the child learns the very opposite of the adult's intention. The message is that aggression is a tactic that the caregiver approves of, because he uses it himself.

Discipline

In dealing with all kinds of misbehaviour it is best to intervene as soon as possible at the start of any undesirable behaviour. This means that the child has to suppress less of the bad behaviour, and often at this stage the emotions involved on both sides are not so strong.

It is also important to explain why the behaviour is undesirable – even though the child may not be paying any attention. The message has to be reinforced by being backed up by an explanation. At some later time, the child herself can use such an explanation as a way of reinforcing her control of her own behaviour, which is a part of her development of self-image and self-regulation.

It is important at the same time as stopping the unwanted behaviour to give the child an alternative and explain why the behaviour is undesirable. By always giving her another way of behaving in a similar situation, eventually the message gets through. 'Instead of kicking Tommy you could have come and asked me to help', for example. Quite often a misbehaviour is unintentional and reflects the limitations of a child's range of responses. She is helped by having other more acceptable ways of responding.

COGNITIVE DEVELOPMENT

Play for development

The amount of time a child spends in role playing and other pretend play usually increases during the pre-school years. There is evidence that a child's tendency to engage in pretend play is related to abilities in aspects of social skills, which are, in turn, related to a child's personality. This can mediate positive links between a child's participation in group pretend and other measures such as performance on role-taking tasks and language abilities.

Pretend play, however, has a direct link with creativity. Children who play more pretend games usually have higher scores on measures of creativity. One measure of creativity is the novel uses test which asks a child to think up as many different ways of using an object as she can. It is easy to see how this would be linked directly to pretend playing, because one aspect of pretending involves substituting one object for another and using objects in new and different ways.

Pretend play is also linked with the ability to solve problems. Research has shown that if children are given an opportunity to play with the objects that are later used for a problem-solving task, then they are able to focus on the task better and solve the problem quicker, with less help. This effect was especially noticeable if the children played with the objects in a pretend manner.

Pretence also needs many cognitive skills such as symbolic representation and understanding of mental states. In fact, these skills appear earlier in pretend play than in other behaviours, indicating that pretend play may be an environment for early competence in cognitive skills as well as in social skills.

Research has shown that pre-schoolers can think more flexibly about a pretend world than about the real world. Their thinking is less tied to what they already know to be true and so they can accept divergence from normal. It can also be more abstract and follow the rules of deductive reasoning rather than being tied to commonsense facts.

Pretend and theory of mind

When tested on false belief tasks, a pre-schooler cannot disengage her own beliefs from those of others – she cannot pass such a task. The task involved watching while a boy hid some chocolate in a cupboard. Then the boy's mother came into the empty room, found the chocolate and put it into a drawer instead. When the boy came back into the room the pre-schooler was asked where the boy would look for his chocolate. Three-year-olds usually say that he will look in the drawer because that is where the chocolate is. They don't understand that the boy can hold the false belief that the chocolate is still in the cupboard where he left it (Flavell et al., 1992).

When a child pretends to be another person, she represents the inner life of that person. She shows she has an understanding of the fact that other people have mental states. This can start as early as two years of age, when a child first attributes 'life' to her doll. Initially, this 'life' is to do with the ability to act, soon after to have desires and intentions, and then emotional and sensory experiences. When she pretends, a child shows that she understands that others have mental states, independent of and sometimes different from her own. Playing in this way may help a child to free her thinking from being tied to self. Experience of pretend games and role

Children start to play with models and miniature worlds at this age. Such a situation encourages children to try out a range of events, relations and feelings in which they are in control of what happens.

play may help the development of those cognitive skills connected with understanding the mental states of others and the development of a child's theory of mind.

Play with models and miniature worlds

In many ways pretend games and playing with small models are similar. A child is, in both cases, playing at fantasy games and entering make-believe worlds. With models and layouts, however, a child is encouraged into a different kind of participation. With pretend in which she uses props, such as dressing up in clothes, a child enters the fantasy as a fully participating member. She becomes the individual character that she is pretending to be. With miniature worlds, a child is more distanced from the action but also in greater control of what can

happen. Pretend games are most often social and group games, whereas, with miniature worlds, a child is more likely to play in a solitary or parallel way. Through such play, a child has the opportunity to try out a wide range of events, relations and feelings in a situation in which she is removed from the action. She has control over the scenario, which means perhaps that she can experiment with more extreme events or emotions. At the same time she is distanced and therefore less disturbed.

A child often plays out ideas from either stories or television when playing with miniature worlds. In her play with models, she is as likely to reveal her current preoccupations or enthusiasms as her anxieties. By pre-school age, a child usually has a wide experience of a variety of story forms, and her play reflects her understanding of fictions and invention as well as real life.

MAKING MODELS FROM JUNK

Collect old packaging for craft work and use in imaginative play. (Expanded polystyrene can be dangerous for young children especially if small pieces are broken off, so caregivers should be careful what kind of junk they collect.)

Large cardboard boxes from washing machines or fridges can make ideal play houses, cars, dens, or whatever a creative child can turn it into using her imagination. She will enjoy painting and decorating it – making doorways or windows, wallpapering the inside or using scraps of material to create curtains. Sometimes a caregiver can tie in such activity with reading a story, for example, 'Hansel and Gretel' and the child could be encouraged to create a candy house, using perhaps paper plate lollipops.

Smaller cardboard packets, egg boxes, plastic bottles and containers, and other packaging can be used by children to stock pretend shops. Children love to play at adult activities such as shopping.

Interesting shaped packaging (including the infamous toilet roll tube) can be used to build junk models by being glued together and then painted. Often younger children will enjoy the process of sticking things together and not really worry about the end-product. As children get older, however, they also enjoy creating something that looks good and give the finished model a label depending on what it ends up looking like. When children get even older they have some idea of what they want to build before they start.

In sequencing the events in her play with miniature worlds, a child learns how to plan and create a story. She is organizing and planning her ideas in a purposeful manner within a playful situation, learning to focus her attention on detail but at the same time keeping an overall scenario and sequence in her head. This ability to focus and shift attention selectively is very important for a child later on in school, where a lot of learning depends on such ability to control her own attention.

First science play with sand, water, clay

A child learns about the different properties of a variety of materials through the hands-on experience of playing. It is also through such play that she learns about which aspects of a substance she can and which she cannot change. This kind of learning paves the way to a child's

knowledge of the world, natural laws and scientific enquiry, as well as specific understanding of, for example, the concept of conservation.

Children learn a lot about science through water play. They learn about science by being curious and testing things out in a practical way. 'What happens if?' is the basic starting point that a curious pre-schooler has in common with a physicist. It is important to encourage such play among children and to provide them with the opportunity and the materials. A variety of empty household containers of various shapes can be useful, for example, they can be pierced in a variety of different ways to provide different sprinkler flows. Plastic containers, jugs and different kinds of floating shapes are also good.

A child learns much about the properties of liquids through direct play with water and a variety of containers and pourers. She also starts to learn about what things float, what sink and what properties floaters share that sinkers do

Through water play, these young scientists are finding out about some of the physical properties of liquids and of objects that do and don't float.

not. This provides the best way for a child to learn basic science, because simply telling a child the information means that it is less likely to be retained. If it is not grounded in her experience, it cannot be integrated into what she already knows. Without such integration a child is likely to forget such information quite quickly.

This doesn't mean, however, that adult input is not needed. As a caregiver already knows the science, he can shape a child's experience and help her focus on the important features, ignoring irrelevant ones. A caregiver can give shape to a child's own explorations and build on her experiences to build up an integrated knowledge base, which can grow as her learning increases. Playing with water is both fun and an important learning situation for a child and this is true at different ages. A young baby gets different things out of water play than a four-year-old. Although carrying out

what looks like the same activity, each is building on a different knowledge base and is learning different things from the experience.

Cooking

One play activity that children can learn a lot from is cooking or baking with a caregiver. Often at nurseries or play groups, this activity is done in groups which is useful for children to learn social skills of turn-taking and sharing. By being undertaken as a group activity, however, a child does not necessarily get a chance to follow through all the steps of the activity directly, with the associated hands-on – or more probably hands-in – experience. Baking at home – where it may be an activity for just a caregiver and one child – can therefore make it a special activity and one that is rich in learning opportunities for the child.

As well as practising general motor skills of pouring, beating, mixing, lifting, etc., a child can also try out particular skills, such as breaking an egg, chopping and cutting up, or sifting flour through a sieve. She can explore the world of mathematics through measuring and weighing and counting, as well as matching, for example, eight cake cases to eight spoons of mixture and eight cherries for the top. If a caregiver explains the process and expands on why the various steps are needed, then a child also gains some insight into chemical processes, hygiene, safety and nutrition. A caregiver can also encourage a child to expand her sensory experience through tasting, smelling and touching the ingredients throughout the process.

Baking is also an ideal way for a child to gain some experience of the concept of planning. The activity can be broken down into steps, with the caregiver explaining why one thing has to happen before another, but after something else. This develops the idea of various steps having an order and sequence: first we wash our hands, then we get out the ingredients, then we light the oven, etc. A child acquires some understanding of planning, ordering and sequencing of tasks.

She also gets direct experience of the sense of the passing of time – she must beat the mixture for one minute, the cake needs to be baked for ten minutes, the cakes may take five minutes to cool, the icing may take ten minutes to set. Timers can be set and clocks monitored to help this learning about time measurement. All this learning takes place within an enjoyable context and has an outcome which gives a great deal of reward so that a child ends up with a feeling of confidence and competence.

As a child gets older, a caregiver might involve her in creating simple picture recipes which show the various steps that they went through to create the end result. This is a way of focusing a child's attention and cultivating her ability to reflect on an experience, as a way of reinforcing the learning that has taken place. It also means that you have some organized material for future use. Drawing such recipes is also a good way of filling the time spent by an impatient and hungry pre-school baker while waiting for things to be ready to eat. As a child

Baking is ideal as an introduction to the concept of planning. This young baker is enjoying herself and also learning about number, shape, sequencing, chemical processes, nutrition, hygiene and safety.

PLAY DOUGH RECIPE

Ingredients
1 cup plain flour
1 cup water
$\frac{1}{2}$ cup of salt
2 teaspoons cream of tartar
1 tablespoon cooking oil
Food colouring

Method 1: Place all ingredients in a saucepan and cook, stirring continuously over a low heat until the mixture thickens to a firm dough texture. This usually takes about five to ten minutes.

Method 2: Place all the ingredients in a container and place in a microwave oven for about one and a half minutes. Stir the mixture and microwave for another minute.

Both methods give a pleasant textured play dough which should last for a few weeks.

SALT DOUGH RECIPE

Ingredients
1 cup of plain flour
$\frac{1}{2}$ cup of salt
1 cup of water

Method: Place dry ingredients in a bowl and add the water gradually. Mix together, then knead until the mixture forms a pliable dough. This dough can be moulded, cut into shapes with biscuit cutters, etc. and then baked in a low oven until hard and dry. Usually this takes up to an hour. When it has been baked the shapes can then be painted and decorated and, if sealed with a clear varnish which keeps out the damp, the shapes will last for ages.

gets older, words and numbers can be incorporated into the recipes. Baking can be expanded to include the shopping for ingredients. Creating a shopping list of pictures and simple words is a good way to introduce a child to the idea of the symbolic function of writing. It can be used as an aid to memory and organizing and representing thoughts. A child can go round the supermarket with her very own list. The drawings help to prompt her memory and she can try to match the words on the list with the words on the packaging.

Making things is very important for children because it gives them a way of empowering themselves. By producing something by themselves, they gain a deep sense of confidence in their own abilities. Making something that is useful adds to their sense of achievement. All children enjoy playing with play dough. As a material it is often more pleasant and easier for young children to handle than Plasticene or clay, but it provides much the same tactile and learning experiences. One added bonus is that, for older children, a dough with a slightly heavier salt content, once moulded or cut into desired shapes, can be baked in the oven, and then painted and varnished to produce durable Christmas tree decorations, beads for necklaces or any number of other decorative objects.

Construction

A child learns a great many things through play with building blocks. Often through play with bricks and building blocks, a child first develops some ideas which then pave the way towards an understanding of number. Such ideas build up with lots of experience using a variety of materials. Sets of bricks give a child experience of *more* and *less*. They introduce some *concept of order* – this tower is taller than that one – and the link between order and number – this tower has more blocks than that one. They also give the *idea of sets* – that some bricks belong together through size or shape. And a rudimentary idea of addition and subtraction

STAGES IN CONSTRUCTION PLAY

1 Exploring: a child plays with the material for itself rather than for what it can make. She plays with how they go together or may use them as collections of small objects. She may play by sorting, collecting and transporting them around.

2 Making a tower: bricks may be stacked on top of each other in a tower.

3 Arranging: a child may line up the bricks next to each other in rows, and then go on to use the blocks to mark off an area by laying the blocks end to end.

4 Bridging: a child uses one block to span two other bricks and thus make a bridge.

5 Patterns: a child uses blocks to create a pattern.

6 Construction: to start with a child may build something and then once it is finished she may give it a name.

7 Planned construction: a child says what she is going to build before she starts constructing it. She is therefore following some inner design or plan and this shapes her activity.

can be developed – if I put on one more brick then it is bigger than before; if I take away a brick then it becomes smaller.

A caregiver should encourage a child to talk about what she is doing when she is playing with bricks. One of the main benefits to learning through such play is the development of the vocabulary to describe mathematical ideas and relationships, and the refinement of such vocabulary. So 'big' may develop to convey more information and become 'tall' or 'wide'. A caregiver can help a child to link her activity to particular words and to build up her vocabulary.

There is a progressive development in the way a child plays with building material such as bricks or blocks.

Drawing and painting

A child's first marks on paper have more to do with the movement of her hand than an attempt to represent the world. Initially, it is the process rather than the end-product that is important. The result of a child's drawing has little meaning for her; she is interested in the experience of learning about the materials and tools rather than trying to create something. It therefore

This young boy is busy painting at home. His level of drawing and painting reflects his cognitive ability and his culture and individual differences.

helps to keep this in mind when providing materials for younger pre-schoolers. They don't keep paints separate because they are interested in finding out what happens when paints are laid one on top of another, or when this colour is mixed with that. Separate brushes for each colour are a good idea. Often a younger child enjoys painting with a single colour and is quite happy with just the one. If you do give more than one colour, then bear in mind the behaviour of the pre-school artist and choose those colours that produce more interesting results when they are inevitably mixed together – for example, blue and yellow giving green. A short brush is easier to handle than a long-handled one. To start with, a child may cover an entire page with paint and then re-paint it with another colour. The child is exploring the medium and not trying to represent anything. She may therefore enjoy covering cardboard boxes with paint or helping to paint in a large background area with colour as much as painting on paper.

The level of drawing does not, however, simply reflect cognitive development. There are various factors related to culture, experience and motor control which influence a child's drawing. Individuals vary greatly in their interest and ability, and there are individual differences in style of drawing within a culture. One study showed that adults could perceive stylistic similarities in individual children's drawings, even over a spread of time. When shown a particular drawing, they attributed it correctly to the child who had done it (Hartley et al., 1982).

Pre-writing skills

When a toddler starts to scribble with a pencil she may be imitating what she sees adults around her doing, which could be drawing or painting, but is more often likely to be writing. From quite early on, some children seem to differentiate between writing and drawing scribbles. Certainly, by pre-school age a child is aware of two separate activities when she is

STAGES IN ART

1 Random marks: a child's first marks with pen or crayon are more of an exploration of cause and effect. She is learning about the properties of pencils, pens, paint, crayons, paper, etc. and about her ability to make things happen.

2 Scribbles: again, these have more to do with extending learning about objects and materials, developing her own motor co-ordination and enjoyment of such movement than in any attempt to represent anything.

3 Basic shapes: growing motor control and hand–eye co-ordination mean that a child can make basic shapes, such as circle, cross, rectangle. She can then combine them to make patterns.

4 Patterns: to start with a child will make a pattern and then interpret her pattern as a representation of something and give it a label; for example, a rectangle and a circle may be called a hat. Often this is something a child learns from an adult.

5 Tadpole people: some patterns that children create come to dominate their drawing for a while. A large circle with lines attached directly as arms and legs becomes a representation of people. A child is drawing what she knows rather than what she sees.

6 Portraits: a child learns to add details such as hair, hands, fingers and feet, and eventually gives the person a body as well.

7 Pictorial drawings: a child's drawing will reflect her interests and her experiences (these will include her experience of looking at art work in books). So she may draw animals, vehicles, houses, trees, plants, flowers, rainbows, etc. She draws what she knows.

scribbling. With writing scribbles, she often mimics many of the features of handwriting – it is usually horizontal, showing that she understands that writing is something that is to be read. A child often pretends to read her own writing scribbles back to herself.

From horizontal scribbles, a child may progress to a kind of mock writing in which her scribbles share some of the features of real handwriting, including a kind of uniformity of size and repetitiveness of shapes. The scribbles may show some elements of symmetry and certain letter-like shapes could emerge.

Writing scribbles should be encouraged. Fine motor control and holding a pencil or pen in a correct grip need a lot of practice. Writing scribbles are a good way of practising and refining such control. Any features of a child's scribbles that are close to real letters should be pointed out by caregivers, named and praised.

The main thing a child is starting to learn is the idea that writing has meaning and that such meaning is communicable. When a child points to a particular patch of scribbles and ascribes meaning, she is making a step on the way to literacy. The one-to-one mapping of scribbles to words shows that she already has an understanding of what writing is all about – she understands the theory but has still to get to grips with the details.

Printing letters

By the age of four, a child may often be able to print some letters or her own name. Capital letters are usually easier for a child because they consist of straight lines. Caregivers should, however, encourage the writing of lower case letters – a child learns greater pencil control by trying to print the curves of these letters and

ART ACTIVITIES

CHILDREN ENJOY A variety of art work. They like to make print pictures with either ink pads and stamps or paint and a collection of different shaped objects, such as corks, Stickle Bricks, Lego bricks, slices of fruit and vegetables, etc. Prints using paint or casts using clay or plaster of her own hands and feet are something that a child enjoys making. She may also enjoy making pictures by gluing things on to paper or card. These can be paper shapes or cut-outs from magazines or old catalogues which she can either cut out with scissors or tear out with her fingers. She enjoys collecting leaves or shells or grasses or flowers to stick on to make pictures. Children enjoy making rubbings and, if a caregiver uses Blu-tack or drawing pins to hold the paper in position over whatever is to be rubbed, then a child should manage to do the rubbing herself. Using salt dough which can later be baked to harden, then painted and varnished, a child can

make beads for threading or play necklaces, counters for games using small biscuit cutters or figures for imaginative play. Again a caregiver can tie such activities to a story book or link them to number and sorting games. With all art activities the aim should be for the child to be able to do as much of the process herself – it is the doing that is more important than the end-product.

they are more useful for a child at school. Lower case letters are the ones that she will come across in her early reading books, so there is less confusion if a child's own writing output reinforces her reading input. The link between shape of letter and sound, which is the corner-stone of literacy, is reinforced.

Often a child can print particular letters, but has a problem with their orientation – she can print a 'p' or a 'b' correctly, but may sometimes have them facing backwards or upside down. She may not understand that there is any difference between a backward or a forward letter, but the way a letter faces does make a great deal of difference, as it becomes something completely different. This is where letters are different from many of the other things that a child has come across. In fact she has had to learn in the past that orientation often does not matter – a brick is a brick at any angle, so it could be hard for a child to grasp that orientation of a letter not only matters but is a crucial part of its identity.

If a child is having problems, she is not necessarily helped by playing with three-dimensional letters which can be put into different orientations. In this scenario, a child is learning about the features of letters, but not necessarily about the way in which they are positioned in space. Even magnetic letters, which can be placed upside down, may add to the confusion if a child is having difficulty.

It is always a good idea for a child who is learning to write her letters to have a handy point of reference – a wall chart or poster – so that she can check her own efforts easily. Such a poster also reinforces her learning not only of the features of letters, but also of their orienta-tion. It can combine correct letter models with pictures as clues to the letter sounds.

Pre-reading skills

A pre-schooler has already learned a number of skills that make learning to read easier. From familiarity with hearing stories and being read to, she has some idea of the sequencing of stories and experience of left-to-right scanning. She has the idea of a left-to-right direction for the unfolding of stories

Recognizing letters

On the whole, children learn to recognize the different letters of the alphabet in a particular sequence. The ability to discriminate different letters depends very much on the features of those letters, for example, a child finds it easier to discriminate straight from round, so the first letter that a child learns to recognize is usually the letter O. A caregiver can help to reinforce the link between shape and the letter sound by making an exaggerated round mouth shape and pointing this out to a child. By encouraging a child to say the sound, feel the shape of her mouth and perhaps look in a mirror at the round O shape her lips make, she soon learns to recognize and name the shape wherever she sees it. A caregiver can turn this into a kind of observation game. In the Western World we are bombarded everywhere with writing and letters, so on a simple outing to the shops a child has lots of opportunities to play 'Spot the O shapes'.

The letter C may also be recognized quite early because of its curved shape, followed by P and S. Again it is helpful for a caregiver to link the shape of an S with the sound of the letter, by using a snake to link the two together. Letters with diagonals, like K and V, are usually recognized later. Although this is one trend, a particular child may learn to recognize letters in a particular sequence for all sorts of different reasons. If her name is Katy, then the diagonal letters K and Y may be learned before the curved ones. A car-mad little boy might learn VW before any others.

The main thing for caregivers to do is to encourage children to observe and discriminate within their own environment. Letters are particular aspects of a child's environment and one on which our modern society places great importance. It is a good idea to encourage a child's natural ability to notice differences and similarities. With letters it helps to give a child a verbal sound hook on which to hang their recognition.

In a similar way, pre-school children also recognize individual words. They may start with their own name and perhaps the words of some road signs: 'Halt' and 'Stop'. Caregivers can build games up around whatever words a child recognizes – either observation games such as 'Can you see the word . . . ?' or by writing the words on flash cards and playing a game of 'A message has arrived for you. I wonder what it says?'. Again the best kind of learning is in the context of a game. Children are experts at picking up on non-verbal signals from those around them. Adult anxiety or pressure can easily become counterproductive in a child's learning.

LANGUAGE DEVELOPMENT

Literacy skills are closely tied to language skills. The child who, in the future, will be a good reader and writer, also has a good speaking vocabulary and can express her thoughts fluently in spoken language.

During the pre-school years and beyond, a child's language continues to develop. She has an expanding vocabulary and at this stage she may be learning new words at the phenomenal rate of up to ten or twenty new words every day. A child is also consolidating much of her learning about the rules of language. This means that she has to revise and reorganize her knowledge and how she stores it. Earlier difficulties with, for example, comparative terms ('bigger') or 'umbrella' terms (words whose meaning implies or includes that of another, e.g. 'animals'), are gradually overcome, as the way she thinks about and organizes her language develops to cope with more complex relationships. A dog can now be a pet and a collie and an animal, all at the same time, without causing the child confusion. The simple one-to-one mapping of a word and what it refers to, which informed the child's early learning, is now superseded. This allows for more complex relationships and mappings between

words. Throughout her primary school years and beyond, a child will continue in this process of learning about and refining her knowledge of language.

Role of adults

Sometimes, the very closeness of communication between a caregiver and a child may hinder the child's development of wider, more generally accessible, language use. They may understand each other too well. It may only be at a nursery or play group that a child comes across some unfamiliar adults, for the first time, and has to learn to adapt her speech in order to be understood. This can be viewed as one way in which an adult helps a child's development by not understanding. Most of the other ways that adults help a child to improve her communication abilities are by trying to see the world from a child's point of view.

An adult can perform a number of important roles in supporting a child's communication throughout the pre-school years and beyond. For example, an adult can define terms and give a child the meanings of words she does not know. He can introduce information at appropriate times and, through knowledge of the child, tailor such information so that she can understand it easily. He can supply prompts to help a child to talk about something or remind her of things she may have forgotten. He can listen to a child, give her close attention, monitor her efforts and give feedback. An adult can help to direct a child's attention to what is relevant and what is not, acting as a filter and interpreter of information to aid her ability to absorb new ideas. Most importantly, however, an adult provides emotional support through encouragement for effort and praise for success. A child who is confident in her ability to communicate her thoughts, needs, wants and feelings already has a head start in terms of ability to succeed in the formal school situation, to master the basic literacy skills, and to gain enjoyment and benefit from the formal learning situation.

CHAPTER SEVEN

THE SCHOOL CHILD

five years upwards

Play continues to be very important for learning and development throughout a child's school years. Often the emphasis after the age of five is on the formal learning situation and other activities are viewed as less important. But even once he is at school, most of a child's learning still takes place in informal play and leisure activities. These activities provide arenas where either particular skills are first encountered or skills encountered in schools are practised, consolidated and mastered.

A child's language continues to develop at this time, in terms of expanding vocabulary and sophistication of usage. It is important to encourage children to strive to express their ideas clearly in language and the best way is to encourage them to engage in conversation with both adults and other children. Through play with other children, they continue to develop their communication skills.

MOTOR DEVELOPMENT
Sport and play

Throughout their school days and beyond children continue to expand and develop their motor skills. Mastery of physical skills motivates a continuing amount of children's play and this is often seen in their enthusiasm for physical games and later for team sports.

Through participation in games and sport, a child gains in strength and stamina as well as developing his physical co-ordination. More and more evidence shows that for healthy development, particularly of the heart, lungs and circulatory system, children need to take part in vigorous physical exercise on a regular basis. This is important for their later long-term health as adults. Playing is the natural way for children to exercise, as in play children are enjoying themselves first and foremost – the physical benefits are secondary. Such enjoyment is probably the best way of ensuring that exercise is part of their daily life both now and in the future. Therefore, it is important for adults to encourage children in physical play, by allowing them the opportunity and providing both time and space for such activity. It is also important that such play is viewed as having value in itself. The older view of play as simply a way to get rid of excess energy, so a child then settles down to his school 'work', does not stand up. The dichotomy of useful work as opposed to purposeless play has been shown to be false. For true development, a child needs both activities to reinforce the learning from each of them.

Team games have the added benefit of encouraging important social skills such as sharing, co-operation, rule observing and a sense of working together towards a common aim. This is in addition to the bursts of physical activity and the motor skills and co-ordination demanded by each game. A child often has to integrate his skills with those of others on his team. He learns to anticipate what his opponents' and team mates' moves might be. Therefore, he needs to hold a degree of planning

Once at school, physical games can be used as a learning medium. Mastery of the physical skills involved motivates a continuing amount of children's play, which leads to continued expansion and development of motor skills.

in his head – both of his own role and of how he might fit into an imagined game. Through playing team games his ability to notice and attend to the actions of others and to co-ordinate his interpersonal skills improves.

The development of motor skills, co-ordination, strength and stamina gained through play has knock-on effects on a child's social and cognitive development. A child who is skilful in one aspect is usually capable in other areas of development. The polarities of 'sporty' versus 'brainy' are on the whole false – at least during the earlier school years. On the contrary, there is evidence that physical and mental development are tied together, although, obviously, there are many individuals who go against this trend.

SOCIAL DEVELOPMENT
Playground games

The playground provides a learning forum for a child's developing social skills. A child learns about himself and others within the give and take of this kind of play activity. He refines his sense of self and understands how individuals behave within a group.

During the early school years, a child makes big strides in his ability to communicate effectively with his peers. In his social interactions, a child is more capable of carrying out his intentions and avoiding unintended breakdowns of communication. He can control his

These young girls are interacting in the playground. This provides a learning forum for their developing social skills.

own behaviour towards others. He modifies his own behaviour in order to achieve certain social goals, for example, he shares in order to be liked by his peers or stops behaving in a particular manner in order to get praise or acclaim from a person whom he admires. He engages with others in friendships based on mutual trust and respect rather than just on participation in common activities.

Friendships

Early friendships are important for a child's later development. They are linked to social adjustment in later life, and this has been shown in one long-term study. Data such as IQ score, school grades, teacher evaluations and peer ratings were collected for a group of eight-year-olds. The same group of children was the subject of a follow-up at the age of nineteen, at which time their mental health records were

checked to see who had needed psychiatric help. It was found that the most effective measure as a predictor of a child's later appearance in the mental health register was his peer rating as an eight-year-old. More than IQ, teacher evaluation or any other measure, how he was seen by his fellow school mates was the only measure that indicated with any accuracy whether he might have later problems needing psychiatric help (Cowen et al., 1973). So the social skills involved in a child's ability to make friends at an early age therefore have an ongoing influence throughout life.

Games with rules

Games of pre-school children often have agreed structures. There may be restraints on how the participants think a child must behave within a particular pretend game, for example, a mummy has to behave in a way that they feel a mummy

Here are two friends in the classroom. It has been found that early friendships are linked to social adjustment in later life. They are important predicators of a child's social development.

should. These kind of constraints can be changed, however, and as rules they count only for the particular participants at that particular time.

As children get older they become more interested in playing the kind of games that have generally agreed rules – such as marbles, or hide and seek. The rules of these games are not so informal, temporary or subject to change. They mean that a game can be started up and played within a short time. The success of the game depends on everyone abiding by the rules. Children know they don't have to spend a long time arguing about how to play the game, they can just get on and play it.

As children become older these kind of more formal games – ones that have a kind of public rule structure – tend to take up a bigger slice of their playtime.

Development of moral reasoning

Based on interviews and observations of children playing the game of marbles, the developmental psychologist, Piaget (1977), was able to draw some conclusions about children's understanding of the meaning of rules. He described three stages, as shown in the box on page 116.

In pretend games, however, even children at a young age have an understanding of the 'rules' of a game as being flexible and agreed among the participants. This may be because, with pretending, the whole game as such is flexible and agreed among the players.

In another of Piaget's methods for finding out what children think about social and moral issues, he gave them a story and asked them to judge between two behaviours and say which was the worse. A boy smashes a whole pile of cups by accident. Another smashes just one cup but does so deliberately. When children were asked to judge them, Piaget found that younger children judge naughtiness by the amount of damage. To smash ten cups is worse than to smash one. After the age of nine, however, children are more likely to take motive or intention into account when judging. At this age, one deliberately smashed cup was judged to be worse than ten accidentally smashed ones.

Other studies have, however, shown that much younger children pay heed to the intention behind a behaviour when judging it. Younger children also seem capable of judging between behaviours that go against social rules – such as spilling things or being untidy – compared with ones that contravene moral rules, such as being selfish or telling lies. The behaviours contravening the moral conventions are viewed as much more serious.

Adult influences

A child's moral thinking is not done in a vacuum or invented from scratch by him. The way he thinks about such issues is influenced by those around him. From a very early age, a child hears adults use the vocabulary of moral approval and disapproval. They talk about and evaluate actions – some things are good, bad, naughty, kind, etc. Children also hear them refer to intentions and motivations as being part of actions and forming part of the way in which

CHILDREN'S UNDERSTANDING OF 'RULES'

Stage 1: up to age five. The rules of a game are not really understood. Children do not keep them consistently.

Stage 2: from age five to ten years. The rules of a game are seen as coming from a higher authority and as such cannot be changed. When playing a game children stick rigidly to the rules.

Stage 3: from the age of ten onwards. Rules are seen as mutually agreed by players. They can therefore be changed by agreement among the players.

(Based on Piaget, 1977)

they judge such actions. A child's development of thinking about social and moral issues is very much tied to the amount of exposure to caregiver elaboration on such matters. If a caregiver talks about why a certain behaviour invites disapproval then he is helping a child to refine and develop his own thinking.

Development of moral behaviour

Young children respond to the distress of others. Babies often cry in direct response to another infant's cry. Older babies also respond to the distress of others, often by needing comfort themselves. Toddlers not only respond to distress but try to help at least some of the time. They either try to comfort the other child or seek help, although often their would-be helpful action may be inappropriate. At this stage a child does not necessarily have the skills needed to respond in the best way to another's distress. They do have a level of social awareness and often want to act in a helpful caring manner towards another.

One of the factors that influences the development of this kind of positive social behaviour is the way caregivers behave. They act as role models for many things, but especially for social behaviours. If a child sees them acting in a helpful, kind, generous, sharing manner, then this makes such behaviours more likely in the child. 'Do as I do' seems to work.

Praising or rewarding a child for any positive social behaviours that he shows, such as sharing or helping somebody, reinforces that kind of behaviour. Explanations also seem to be effective in influencing a child's behaviour. If an adult explains to a child about the consequences of his actions, then this reinforces any learning of positive social behaviours.

A child is more likely to repeat a generous act if he has seen an adult act in a similar way, if he is rewarded for such behaviour by praise or if an adult explains to him why it is a good idea to act in this way.

This method of combining positive

reinforcement with a cognitive explanation of the consequences of one's actions is probably the most effective form of teaching a child how to behave. It is associated with a greater maturity in terms of both reasoning and behaviour among children, when compared with other forms of disciplining a child, such as asserting power or physical punishment.

Learning from television

School-age children spend a large portion of their leisure time watching television. With some children, it can be up to five hours or more every day, which, including weekends, means that they spend longer in front of the television than they do in the classroom.

What do they learn?

The answer is, of course, that they learn a wide spectrum of things from television – some are excellent and educational and, at the other extreme, is mindless violence and stereotypical views and attitudes. The content of what a child learns can be varied and caregivers have to take responsibility for their own children's viewing.

After all parents know their own child best and, especially with younger children, it may be that a child has a particular fearful response to something that another child finds completely inoffensive and harmless.

Children derive many beneficial educational experiences from television. It can widen the horizons and introduce them to aspects of learning and experiences that they would never experience otherwise. The whole wide world is brought into their living rooms. In this respect television performs some of the same functions as books – television as a kind of 'super-book'. It can act as a kind of encyclopaedia or a source of factual information, but in a way that children may find more compelling because of the vividness of the medium. Watching lions hunt in Africa in a television programme is more immediate and engaging of a child's attention. It also takes less effort on the part of a child, however, than reading about it. With a book a child has to decode the messages and use his imagination.

As a kind of 'super story-book', television performs the function of fiction and make-believe that was previously performed solely by

Television plays a role in the life of these school-age children. It is known that such children spend a large portion of their leisure time watching television, so it is important that their viewing is monitored and used to help them learn positively.

books (and earlier still by an oral tradition). This is television as entertainment. This is not an unimportant aspect of life as entertainment can also provide a good learning environment. With the best quality television programmes, there is no division between entertainment and education. Educational programmes entertain in order to get their message across and entertainment programmes stimulate learning and provoke thought. For beginning readers, it is perhaps a good idea to use television subtitles to reinforce the link between words and meaningful pictures and to create a context in which words form part of a story form.

The area in which television's influence may not be so beneficial is the one in which it stops children from doing other things. Informal play – with its benefits of physical exercise and social skills development – may be limited if too much leisure time is spent in front of the television set.

Similarly, because it takes less effort to watch a television programme than to read a book, a child may read a lot less. As with all skills, the less they are practised the less they are mastered. A child who does very little reading, apart from the unavoidable stuff at school, does not exactly forget how to read, but does not perhaps develop the speed and fluency that is needed if reading is ever to become something other than a chore. There is a certain level of ease and speed in the actual process of reading that a child has to acquire, if he is to be able to understand the ideas, concepts and information that a book holds. Sometimes it can be a case of being unable to see the wood for the trees, that is, a child can get bogged down in the words if he has to take too much time over processing them and does not understand the ideas that the words are trying to convey. Lots and lots of practice in reading to improve and speed up the process is the only answer.

Reading a lot for pleasure has knock-on effects on a child's own writing skills, vocabulary size and spelling. So if a child does not read outwith school, then presumably this has an effect. Literacy skills are integrated – reading,

This boy is doing something that should be encouraged. Reading a lot for pleasure has benefits for a child's own writing skills and vocabulary size.

writing, listening and talking. Each works on the others. Television watching may stop children reading for pleasure and also have an effect on the amount of conversation within the home. Watching a lot of television is often linked to reduced social interaction and conversation. Communication and talking skills should be encouraged throughout a child's life, not just when he is acquiring the basics of language.

Models

The content of some television programmes may also be teaching children behaviours and giving them ideas that are not those that an adult wants for the child. This is where adults have to be vigilant about the content of programmes. They must be aware of what messages are being given out and also what messages are being receiving by the children. The two might not be the same thing – especially if a programme is aimed at adults. What children may understand from a programme might not be what the programme maker intended and not what an adult viewer might understand. It is important that television programmes are discussed, especially if they are presenting ideas or messages that a child has no experience of in his day-to-day life. Research has shown that children are most influenced by television portrayals that are not subject to the modifying influences of their own experience or caregivers' views and ideas, and therefore have not been put into perspective. Two areas in which television portrayals usually have greater weight and influence are sex and violence, as children do not usually have any other sources of information or experience to modify or put television's portrayal into perspective.

Violence

It has been shown that, for some especially vulnerable individuals, the portrayal of acts of violence on television can act as a model that they may copy. Among the general population, there is a great deal of debate about the effects of television violence on violent and aggressive behaviour. There does not seem to be a clear answer one way or the other, and there is definitely no simple answer.

Some studies do show that television can affect social behaviour, although the relationship is subject to other intervening variables which make it hard to disentangle causes and effects.

One study tried to ascertain whether violent television makes people aggressive or whether instead naturally aggressive people just like to watch violent television. In this study, boys were studied at age nine and nineteen, and the aggression was based on a rating given by their peers (Lefkowitz et al., 1977).

The outcome of this study suggested that the relationship is between watching violent television and later aggression, rather than an early aggression leading to later liking for violent television. Watching violent television does have some influence on later behaviour.

A critical viewer

This finding has strong implications for those involved with young children. It reinforces the idea that television programmes must be monitored for content. Caregivers also have to take some responsibility for modifying the strength of television's influence by their own input. A particular portrayal or programmes should be talked about, argued over, etc. In a way, a caregiver has to teach a child to become a critical viewer – aware of television as a medium and able to develop a degree of cynicism towards the variety of messages that he receives through that medium. Advertising is one area where it is probably in a caregiver's best interest to aid such development in the child as soon as possible.

How do they learn?

With television, the message comes in attractive colourful packaging. It uses aural and visual channels – music, speech and moving image. It has built up expertise in how to grab attention and keep it, through the timing of changing images and the pace of delivery. Television is therefore a very powerful and seductive medium. With television, however, a child is very much the passive recipient of information. The thrust of modern educational theory has been to emphasize the necessity of children becoming active in their own learning. Hands-on experience by the child is seen as an important way for him to fix his learning by grounding it in his own experience. So, perhaps television is not the most effective medium for learning for young children. It may have an immediate impact and short-term influence, but be less successful in fostering long-term acquisition of knowledge and learning.

Children often watch television when they are very relaxed or sleepy so that they are not very alert and attentive, which actually helps the child to take in and remember information from television.

Research has shown that children don't remember much of what they have viewed on television even on the previous night. The more programmes they watch the less they remember about the content of individual programmes.

COGNITIVE DEVELOPMENT
Learning and computer play

There are many aspects of computers that children find appealing. They share many of the attractions of television in terms of having features which compel attention in a variety of modes. Unlike television, however, a child is not passive. Whether playing a computer game or using a computer program a child is engaging directly with the computer.

A pre-schooler who is allowed access to a computer usually explores it in a similar way to how he explores other things in his environment. He plays around with the program, making mistakes, trying again and eventually figuring out what to do. This hands-on approach can be an effective method of self-learning. In many ways, it can be a much better attitude towards learning than an adult often has when first introduced to something new. Adults are often inhibited from trying out something for fear of failing. They find it hard to cope with the feeling of not knowing what is going on, and also fear losing face by showing their lack of knowledge. It is therefore a good idea for new technologies to be introduced before this kind of self-consciousness gets in the way of learning.

There are many computer games and programs for even the youngest of children to play or participate in. Being able to read or recognize some letters is not a prerequisite for a child to interact with a computer. With the concept keyboard, a child does not have to be able to recognize the letters of the traditional keyboard, but can engage simply by pressing on pictures or symbols. By using a mouse a child can click on to symbols or pictures on the screen or draw directly by moving the mouse.

In primary schools, many computer games give children practice in, for example, using multiplication tables. As the game is enjoyable, the child is getting practice without getting bored. This is an especially good way of aiding children who may need extra revision of previous learning or extra practice. Computers can help with testing how well a child has learned something without the anxiety of a formal exam situation.

Problem solving is an area also addressed by much computer software. The problems are often embedded in fantasy games which engage the children's interest, but they require as much mental effort as those presented in a more traditional manner.

Word processing on a computer can be used as a way of encouraging the language skills of those children whose handwriting and letter forming are, for one reason or another, very slow. If it is something that they find difficult, often the chore of writing puts them off attempting to re-draft a piece of work. They prefer to keep something that is at a lower level of competence than they are capable of producing. Word processing can encourage self-criticism, error spotting, and correction and re-drafting as a natural and important part of writing. By making it less of an effort, and more interesting, children are encouraged to work on a piece of writing to make it better.

Similarly, a computer can aid design and art work during the school years. Often a child's critical abilities are in advance of his physical co-ordination or ability to produce something that he finds satisfying. Use of a computer design package could help him to produce high quality work and keep an interest in art, at a time when his own self-criticism might mean his interest starts to wane.

With both writing and art, however, the computer is used as an adjunct to a child's continuing practice of the writing and drawing process. It doesn't substitute for the art or

Computers are a good tool for self-learning, again with monitoring of the programs used. They can help to bring fun into the practice of basic arithmetic skills.

writing activity but is merely another tool that a child can use at certain times.

Board games

Games, such as Ludo, Snakes and Ladders, Monopoly, Scrabble and Cluedo, have been family favourites for years. Children enjoy playing them very much. These games also provide a child with practice in basic skills of counting, adding, reading, writing and concentration, as well as in problem solving and strategic thinking. Unlike similar practice with

computer games, such play is not solitary so at the same time it provides a forum for talking and listening, and for reinforcing social skills, such as turn-taking and patience. One great bonus is that it is an activity that adults and children play together. By school age activities are often segregated into age ghettos. Although much of this is natural and reflects a child's growing independence from adults, it seems a shame that a great deal of the communicative bond between child and caregiver, which has been built up so carefully throughout a child's early life, can start to disintegrate. Shared activities are one way of keeping open the channels of communication when busy lives and differing schedules mean that less time is spent in each other's company.

Development of abstract thinking skills

Over the course of his school days a child's thinking skills develop. He comes to understand many concepts, and is also able to follow a line of reasoning and to weigh up arguments. Psychologists have identified many features of this development towards what we consider mature adult thought.

One trend during the early school years is the movement away from *animism*. A younger child tends to attribute feelings and intentions to inanimate objects. As a child gets older, he can discriminate between animate and inanimate objects, and realize that only animate objects have feelings.

Another trend at this time is away from ideas that are bound up in context towards ideas that are context free. This is seen in a child's use of language which develops from being, on the whole, initially a private communication between two people with a shared context. This shared context gives the communication much of its meaning so that it does not make sense to uninvolved others. As a child develops, his communication becomes less reliant on context for meaning and therefore becomes open to understanding by people in general. In a similar way, there is a developmental trend in a child's thinking skills from thought that is concrete and embedded in specific contexts towards thinking that is more abstract and disembedded.

At this stage, another trend is the development of a child's ability to be less egocentric. A young child exhibits *egocentrism* which is a view of the world that is centred on himself, so that he finds it hard to take the perspective of another person. This refers to his cognitive skills rather than his social ones. It is not the same thing as being selfish, but refers to a child's inability to take the viewpoint of another in a perceptual way. As a child gets older, he is able to *decentre*, that is, attend to more than one feature of a problem at a time. So he can hold his own perspective, but at the same time see another's point of view.

Conservation

At this time a child acquires the ability to *conserve*, which is a cognitive skill in which a child understands that certain properties of an object remain the same despite changes in the object's appearance. For example, the same lump of clay weighs the same whether it is rolled into a ball or flattened into a pancake. Up until school age, a child does not usually understand that the clay does not actually become *more* by being moulded into a bigger shape. This is where experience through play with materials, such as clay, Plasticene or dough, can be a valuable part of learning. It is only through hands-on experience that a child gradually gains an understanding of such a concept.

There are different kinds of conservation: mass, liquid, number. Although the underlying idea is the same for the different kinds, a child doesn't grasp all of them at the same time. As a child's thinking is still embedded within a context and is concrete rather than abstract, each kind of conservation is viewed as a different problem to be solved. He doesn't perceive the underlying principle and apply it to other similar tasks.

Conservation of a liquid is when a child sees that the amount of a liquid remains the same even when it is poured into a container of a different shape. For a younger child, when the same volume of liquid is poured from a tall thin container into a short fat one, it is likely to be judged as less than it was before. Again hands-on experience of playing with water and a variety of containers helps a child to develop his understanding of conservation of volume.

With number, the child has to learn that a

This boy is learning about the concept of conservation of mass through his play with clay. Other materials that can be used include Plasticene and dough.

certain number of objects remains the same even when the individual objects are spread out and so look larger. A younger child is usually distracted from the number by paying attention to the spacing. For example, he might agree that, with two separate groups of objects, there are more of one group than of the other. Then if the group with fewer objects is spread out and he is asked again, the child is likely to say that this group now has more than the other.

Class inclusion

Young children have difficulty with the idea of classes and categories that are not at the same level of description. For example, the idea of all dogs also being animals but not all animals being dogs is quite a tricky relationship for children to handle. The idea of classes and

subsets is something that children develop only through time and experience. Whether a child has gained this kind of understanding can be tested by specific tasks. A child is asked to sort farm animals into two groups of, say, five horses and three cows. Then he is asked whether there are more horses or more animals. A younger child focuses on the larger group of horses and says that there are more horses than animals. This is even after what is meant by 'animals' has been discussed.

Problems with the tasks that test conservation

Nowadays, there is general agreement that children may learn to conserve much earlier than was previously thought. Although, for some, this is not until the age of seven or eight, for many children they first exhibit the ability to understand the concept of conservation during their pre-school years.

This change results from problems with the traditional tasks designed to test whether a child can conserve or not. Often the language used was difficult and led to misunderstanding by a child. If a child misunderstands the tasks then we don't know whether he can conserve or not. Children are also usually experts at looking for clues as to how to behave. Social referencing, whereby an infant looks to his mother for clues as to how to behave, is an early developmental strategy. In a test situation that is strange to a child, he looks for clues of how to behave from the adults around him. The adults in the conservation task situations either do not help or, through the phrasing of their questions, actually give completely unhelpful clues.

In a way, the testers who designed the tasks were exhibiting a lack of decentring themselves. They were focusing on that aspect of the task which isolated the particular thinking skill to be tested, without taking into account the perspective of the child.

Training

The ability of a child to understand conservation is often seen as something that he comes to through a natural process of experience and development. Children can, however, also be taught or trained successfully. For example, if a child is helped in the tasks by an adult focusing his attention on the right attribute and not letting him become distracted by irrelevant attributes, then he can perform conservation tasks successfully at a much younger age. A child who cannot conserve can do so, after such training.

It has been found, however, that trained children are not as sure of themselves as those who have arrived at the ability through natural development. If they are confronted by something that seems to go against conservation, then they revert to their previous beliefs. For example, children who were trained to conserve were exposed to some trickery. A small piece was

pinched off a ball of clay; earlier they had come to see, through training, that this clay stayed the same no matter what its shape. When the trained children saw that it did after all weigh less, they reverted to their previous belief – that a tight ball of clay weighed less than the same clay flattened into a bigger shape. Natural conservers, that is, children who had arrived at the stage of understanding conservation through their development rather than from specific training, however, when confronted by the evidence of the scales reacted with a great deal of surprise. It seemed to go against a strongly held belief of theirs, and over half of these children thought either that the scales were wrong or that a piece of clay must have fallen off unseen, etc. They were convinced that their belief as regards conservation was correct despite evidence to the contrary.

Divergent thinking

As well as developing logical thought, children start to show abilities to bring together a variety of disconnected ideas. This kind of thinking is associated with creativity in problem solving or in coming up with new ideas. It has been found that children who engage in a lot of pretend play also engage in divergent thinking.

Divergent thinking can be fostered by giving open-ended play materials rather than things that can be used only in one particular way. This allows a child to play around with a variety of different ideas and to use his imagination. For example, construction sets that are flexible and can be built into a variety of different objects foster creativity more than sets that can be used to build only one particular model.

This kind of open-ended imaginative play leads children not only to perform better on divergent thinking tasks, but to perform better on tasks in which focused convergent thinking is required, such as solving puzzles. Not only does playing have benefits for creative thinking, these benefits are transferred across the board into more traditional thinking domains.

BIBLIOGRAPHY

Angelin S. and Lillard A.S. (1993). Pretend play skills and a child's theory of mind. *Child Development* 6: 348–371.

Beaty J (1994). *Observing the Development of the Young Child*. Oxford: Maxwell Macmillan.

Belsky J., Goode M. and Most R. (1980). Maternal stimulation and infant exploratory competence. *Child Development* 51: 1163–1178.

Bower T. (1977). *A Primer of Infant Development*. San Francisco, CA: Freeman.

Bruner J., Jolly A. and Sylva K. (eds) (1976). *Play: Its Role in Development and Evolution*. Harmondsworth: Basic Books.

Clark E. (1982). Language change during language acquisition. In: *Advances in Developmental Psychology*, Vol 2 (Lamb M. and Brown A., eds). Hillsdale, NJ: Erlbaum.

Cohen D. (1987). *The Development of Play*. London: Croom Helm

Cooper R. and Aslin R. (1994). Developmental differences in infant attention to the spectral properties of infant directed speech. *Child Development* 65: 1663–1677.

Cowen E., Pederson A., Babigian H., Izzo L. and Trost M. (1973). Long term follow up of early detected vulnerable children. *Journal of Consulting and Clinical Psychology* 41: 438–446.

Crompton R. (ed.) (1989). *Computers and the Primary Curriculum*. London: Falmer Press

De Casper A. and Fifer W. (1980). Of human bonding: newborns prefer their mothers' voices. *Science* 208: 1174–1176.

Dennis W. and Dennis M. (1940). Effects of cradling practices on the onset of walking in Hopi children. *Journal of Genetic Psychology* 56: 77–86.

Doyle A., Connolly J. and Rivest L. (1980). Effects of playmate familiarity on the social interactions of young children. *Child Development* 51: 217–223.

Fein G. (1981). Pretend play in childhood. *Child Development* 52:1095–1118.

Fernald A. (1993). Approval and disapproval: infant responsiveness to vocal affect in familiar and unfamiliar languages. *Child Development* 64: 657–674.

Flavell J., Mumme D., Green F. and Flavell E. (1992). Young children's understanding of different types of beliefs. *Child Development* 63: 960–977.

Garton A. (1992). *Social Interaction and the Development of Language and Cognition*. Hove: Lawrence Erlbaum Associates.

Gesell A. and Thomson H. (1929). Learning and growth in identical infant twins: an experimental study by the method of co-twin control. *Genetic Psychology Monographs* 6: 1–124.

Gleitman H., Newport A. and Gleitman L. (1984). The current status of the Motherese Hypothesis. *Journal of Child Language* 11: 43–79.

Greenfield P.M. (1984). *Mind and Media*. London: Fontana.

Harris M. (1992). *Language Experience and Early Language Development*. Hove: Lawrence Erlbaum Associates.

Hartley V., Somerville S., Jensen D. and Eliefja C. (1982). Abstraction of individual styles from the drawings of five year old children. *Child Development* 53: 1193–1214

Kaye K. (1982). *The Mental and Social Life of Babies*. London: Methuen.

Laishley J. (1987). *Working with Young Children*. London: Edward Arnold.

Lefkowitz M., Eron L., Walder L. and Huesmann L. (1977). *Growing Up to be Violent*. New York: Pergamon Press.

Light P., Sheldon S. and Woodhead M. (1991). *Learning to Think*. Milton Keynes: Open University Press.

Lilliard A. (1993). Young children's conceptualization of pretence-action or mental representational state? *Child Development* 64: 372–386.

Lorenz K. (1971). *Studies in Animal and Human Behaviour*, Vol 2, pp. 173–174. Boston, MA: Harvard University Press.

McCune-Nicolich S. (1981). Towards symbolic functioning: structure of early pretend games and potential parallels with language. *Child Development* 52: 785–797.

Meltzoff A. and Borton R. (1979). Intermodal matching by human neonates. *Nature* 282: 403–404.

Meltzoff A. and Moore M. (1983). Newborn infants imitate adult facial gestures. *Child Development* 54: 702–709

Newson J. and Newson E. (1979). *Toys and Playthings*. Harmondsworth: Penguin.

Ochs E. and Schefflin B. (1984). Language acquisition and socialization: Three developmental stories and their implications. In: *Culture and Its Acquisition* (Schweder R. and Levine R., eds). Chicago: University of Chicago Press.

Parten M. (1932). Social participation among pre-school children. *Journal of Abnormal and Social Psychology* 27: 243–269.

Piaget J. (1977). *The Moral Judgement of the Child*. Harmondsworth: Penguin.

Quinn J. and Rubin K. (1984). The play of handicapped children. In: *Child's Play: Developmental and Applied* (Yawkey T. and Pellegrini A., eds). Hillsdale, NJ: Lawrence Erlbaum Associates.

Reddy V. (1991). Playing with others' expectations: Teasing and mucking about in the first year. In: *Natural Theories of Mind* (Whiten A., ed.). Oxford: Basil Blackwell.

Riddick B. (1982). *Toys and Play for the Handicapped Child.* London: Croom Helm.

Robson B. (1989). *Preschool Provision for Children with Special Needs (Special Needs in Ordinary Schools).* London: Cassell Educational.

Savelsbergh G. and Van der Kamp J. (1994). Effect of body orientation on early infant reaching. Journal of Experimental *Child Psychology* 58: 510–528.

Seifert K. and Hoffnung R. (1991). *Child and Adolescent Development.* Boston, MA: Houghton Mifflin.

Smith P. and Cowie H. (1988). *Understanding Children's Development.* Oxford: Basil Blackwell.

Stern D. (1984). Mother and infant at play. In: *The Effect of the Infant on its Caregiver* (Lewis M. and Rosenblum L.A., eds). New York: Wiley Interscience.

Tamis-LeMonda C., Damast A. and Bornstein M. (1994). What do mothers know about the developmental nature of play. *Infant Behaviour and Development* 17: 341–345.

Thomas A. and Chess S. (1978). Temperamental individuality from childhood to adolescence. *Annual Progress in Child Psychiatry and Child Development* 66: 223–244

Trevarthen C. and Logotheli K. (1989). Child and culture. In: *Cognition and Social Worlds* (Gellatly A., Rogers D. and Sloboda J., eds). Oxford: Oxford University Press

Underwood J. and Underwood G. (1990). *Computers and Learning.* Oxford: Basil Blackwell

Werker J. and Tees R. (1985). Cross language speech perceptions – evidence for perceptual re-organization during the first year of life. *Infant Behaviour and Development* 7: 49–63.

White B. (1975). *The First Three Years of Life.* Englewood Cliffs, NJ: Prentice-Hall.

Yawkey T. and Pellegrini P. (eds) (1984). *Child's Play: Developmental and Applied.* New York: Lawrence Erlbaum Associates.

Zelazo N. and Zelazo P. (1972).Walking in the new-born. *Science* 176: 314–315.

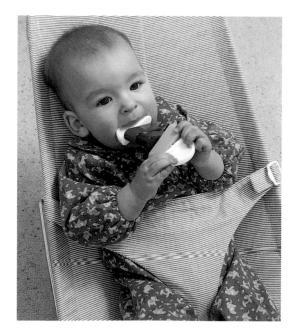

INDEX